DELAWARE'S GHOST TOWERS
Third Edition

The Coast Artillery's Forgotten Last Stand
During the Darkest Days of World War 2

WILLIAM C. GRAYSON

authorHOUSE

AuthorHouse™
1663 Liberty Drive
Bloomington, IN 47403
www.authorhouse.com
Phone: 833-262-8899

First edition published in 2005. Second edition published in 2008.

Published by AuthorHouse 11/17/2021

ISBN: 978-1-6655-4236-4 (sc)
ISBN: 978-1-6655-4237-1 (e)

Library of Congress Control Number: 2021921855

Includes bibliographical references and index.
1) World War 2 – History. 2) Artillery – History.   3) US Army – History.
4) German Navy – History. 5) Coast Artillery Museum.

Print information available on the last page.

This book is printed on acid-free paper.

Also by William C. Grayson:

- *Beefstew Saves Lives on D-Day, A Young Flier Thinks Outside the Box to Dramatically Reduce Casualties at Normandy, ISBN 978-1-4958-2146-2*

- *Delaware's Ghost Towers, The Coast Artillery's Forgotten Last Stand During the Darkest Days of World War 2, 1ˢᵗ and 2ⁿᵈ Editions, ISBN 978-0-7414-4906-4*

- *At Least I Know I'm Free, How Americans Could Have Lost Their Freedoms, ISBN 0-7414-4036-9*

- *Chicksands: A Millennium of History, 1ˢᵗ, 2ⁿᵈ, and 3ʳᵈ Editions, ISBN 0-9633208-1-5*

- *Ear on the War in Vietnam and Presidential Visit, two chapters included in the book, These Guys, ISBN 0-9670169-4-0*

- *Chicksands: The Battle of Britain and the Blitz, Shefford Press*

- *Article: WWII Museums – Fort Miles, Delaware, published in Military Magazine*

- *Two Book Reviews: The Price of Vigilance and Secret War, published in Military Magazine*

- *A Double Book Review: Scorpion Down and All Hands Down in The Phoenician (Journal of NSA retirees)*

- *Article: China, Iran and North Korea Filling Vacuums, published in Military Magazine*

- *Two Chapters: Headquarters Closure and Filling Sandbags published by McManmon Associates in New Ideas in Management*

- *Textbook: Introduction to Communications Security, Computer Security Institute*

- *Textbook: Securing Computer Centers, MIS Training Institute*

Preface

Delaware's Atlantic coast from Cape Henlopen to Fenwick Island offers its string of "quiet resorts" that draw great numbers of vacationers from Washington and nearby eastern states. Paralleling the shore, State Route 1 is the only north-south highway connecting all of Delaware's ocean resort towns and unavoidably exposes travelers to a stand of mysterious towers that evoke questions about them and, unfortunately, have given rise to tenacious myths borne of guesswork.

As a frequent visitor to the area, I am among those who wondered about the towers for years and was frustrated by the dearth of available information about them. All of the towers are on ground designated as state park land, with the majority situated in Cape Henlopen State Park, near the town of Lewes. Through 2004, the book shop in the park's Visitor Center did not offer any printed details of the towers' history. The shop's staff was unable to recommend a book or pamphlet, explaining that an earlier text was contaminated by error, was out of print, and not for sale. Confronted by that challenging vacuum and the wish that "somebody" ought to research and publish the historical details, I succumbed to the same lures that led me earlier to be the "somebody" who wrote the history of an obscure, super-secret site in England.[1]

As I learned researching that earlier history, completed in 1991, important places are made important by significant human events, which almost always are complicated by protagonists versus antagonists, decisions made difficult by sobering restraints, planning needs, priorities for managing scarce resources, and a desire for success rather than unacceptable failure. Fort Miles is one such important place and the fort's most visible reminders are its mysterious ghost towers, souvenirs of one of the most fearful periods of modern American history.

The towers hint of a larger story worth understanding and memorializing. Although the most easily glimpsed, the towers' purposes are part of an unseen larger picture that includes the Army's biggest guns of World War 2, sophisticated underwater defenses, seagoing soldiers, and searchlight crews. I am grateful for the opportunity to have pulled its many complicated details together and to share

---

[1] Chicksands in Bedfordshire

them with readers, who may be interested in a little-known and poorly- understood vignette of modern American history that deserves celebration, especially by visitors to the Delaware seashore.

In particular, America's young people, accustomed to the modern marvels and conveniences of life since the end of the Cold War, will find that the events to which Fort Miles responded are useful for comprehending our newly-changed world in which the patterns of daily life are threatened by barbarous terrorism and electronic aggression. Although the term wasn't in use when Fort Miles' towers were operational, the towers and the fort's other assets were critical Homeland Defense resources. I have also tried to draw attention to the routines and non-combat sacrifices of Army life at Fort Miles during World War 2 and to acknowledge the contributions made by young soldiers, who have tended, modestly, to minimize them.

I am indebted in a major way to the Coast Defense Study Group (CDSG), who publish scholarly historical research on coastal forts, artillery guns and their support equipment. CDSG preserves and offers a wealth of pertinent information via their website at *cdsg.org*. One of its members, Elliot Deutsch, helped me interpret the intricacies of artillery targeting and fire control. The late Lee Jennings, Delaware State Parks Historian and the staff of the Cape Henlopen State Park administrative office made valuable information sources available for study.

Dr. Gary Wray, President Emeritus of the Fort Miles Historical Association, contributed valuable insights and corrections to the draft. The book's research was also much helped by archivists at the Library of Congress, the US Army Artillery Museum at Aberdeen Proving Grounds, the National Archives, the Lewes Historical Society, and the Rehoboth and Lewes Public Libraries.

At almost every turn searching for answers to questions beginning, "Why," I found it necessary to learn underlying or related subject matter and discovered more than I could ever have imagined was so readily available on numerous websites as well as in many good books. I have credited the more important of these in the "End Notes" at the back of the book for those who may be curious about additional details. USAF Colonel Vic Brown and USMC Lieutenant Colonel Clarke Ansel, both serious students of geo-political and military history, reviewed the draft for readability and provided a critical review. Captain William J. Malicki/US Navy Intelligence and LCDR Web Wright/Instructor of History/US Naval Academy assessed the book's two Alternative History scenarios (Annexes D-1 and D-2) for plausibility.

Dr. Frank Sledge and my son, John W. Grayson, an artillerist reenactor, checked the mathematical examples used to explain the roles of the towers and artillery fire control. Professor Dean Wheeler of Brigham Young University helped me with calculations of artillery projectile apogees and times of flight. Tom Kramer collected most of the photos from the Library of Congress and National Archives. The late Lee Jennings helped to obtain photos held by Delaware Public Archives and generously shared his own collected papers and maps. Margaret Newman filled in the blanks on the towers at Cape May, New Jersey. My wife, Shirley, shared a great many research visits to all the towers and gun emplacements and generously tolerated my dedication to long periods of reading, writing, and rewriting.

In the American West, occasional towns bypassed by economic fortune were abandoned by their inhabitants and have come to be known as "ghost towns." In this context, I see Delaware's coastal towers as "ghosts." Without suggesting that they are haunted, it is nonetheless possible to imagine Fort Miles' towers, bunkers, and gun emplacements populated by GIs, edgy about what might be approaching beyond the horizon but solemnly pledged to stand together and defend American soil. This book is dedicated to those who served in the Coast Artillery at all the forts on America's shores.

Washington

Table of Contents

Foreword

There is a sobering aspect of military service that separates it absolutely from all other human callings. Military personnel swear an oath of obedience to orders, even if such obedience inconveniences or tires them, preempts important personal plans, jeopardizes their businesses, diminishes their livelihoods, interrupts their educations, removes them from families who need them at home, sends them to terrible places for long times, and places them at very serious risk of life and limb. Under certain circumstances, violation of the oath may be punishable by death and, in all circumstances, places the violator at risk of criminal punishment, a feature of military service unique among occupations. In most other human activities – professional, social, educational, recreational – competing personal priorities work to restrict levels of individual participation in those other activities and an activity may be modified or abandoned altogether, for higher priorities, if it stops being fun, becomes too expensive, or if anyone were to be seriously hurt.

The Coast Artillery Corps

During World War 2, when the US needed to protect strategic shorelines from enemy seaborne attack, soldiers of the Army's Coast Artillery Corps, under the standard oath of obedience, manned a round-the-clock front line combat- ready watch at forts on all three American coastlines. In the ominous days of 1941 and 1942, a militarily unprepared Nation could not confidently discount having to repel enemy invaders of US coastal waters or, worse, east coast beaches.

In common with young Americans from all 48 states and US territories, soldiers of the Coast Artillery Corps – drawn from state National Guards and the Regular Army – devoted themselves completely to their assignments, ready to follow their orders regardless of any dangers they might face

A heavy artillery piece must be served by a large crew of well-trained soldiers, if the piece is to maintain a sustained rate of effective fire and support the accomplishment of the unit's mission, for the Coast Artillery Corps, repelling an enemy attack from the sea. The whole crew must go to and remain at battle stations immediately when ordered to do so, forsaking all other distractions. If US coastal guns had been needed to engage approaching enemy ships or aircraft, Coast Artillerymen in many assignment specialties would have been ordered to stand and fight, many performing their duties in the open air, exposed to enemy naval bombardment or aerial attack, just where the enemy would be expected to aim suppressive fire.

Despite the obvious vulnerability to lethal enemy fire, these soldiers could not have sought shelter in bunkers, trenches or foxholes; neither could they have fled the fort for safer areas not under attack. An illustrative example comes down to us from World War I. In August of 1917, Artillery Battery D of the Army's 35th Division was firing at German targets in the Vosges Mountains of France when accurate German counter-battery rounds began falling close to the Americans' 75mm gun emplacements. An NCO panicked and shouted for the cannoneers to run and the men began abandoning their positions. The battery commander, Captain Harry Truman, was on a horse, which was hit by shrapnel and went down, pinning and nearly crushing him. Out from under the horse, Truman began yelling profanity-spiced orders for the gunners to get back to their battle stations. They complied and continued the fight.

US Army artillery gun crew comes out of their sandbag shelter running to battle stations

Personal protective gear of the World War 2 era was limited to a steel helmet and a gas mask, if one was at hand. Searchlight crews at water's edge, pointing a bright beam out to sea, figuratively told an enemy warship, "Here I am," and they stayed in place, protected only by a low wall of sandbags. Artillery observers' concrete towers would have been the most prominent aiming points for German gunnery officers offshore and the troops manning the towers would have had to stay at their posts during a naval bombardment. This is the rawest concept of "warfighting" and among the toughest tests of individual loyalty to one's military oath to follow orders.

A great number of factors dissuaded enemy forces from attempting to penetrate American inland waterways or to come ashore on ocean beaches. However, at the outset of World War 2, neither scenario was implausible and the National Guardsmen and their US Army counterparts could never know with certainty that they would not be called upon to fight at a moment's notice. True to their oaths, they stood in the fort, ready for duty, till given leave. They practiced and honed their skills and teamwork. They worked with dangerous explosives, moved very heavy munitions and equipment, and constantly cleaned and maintained everything they came in contact with in their batteries, billets, mess halls and motor pools.

At Coast Artillery forts, no medals were won for valor and no Purple Hearts were awarded. Still, the big guns and their crews were kept at the ready. Looking back, some of the Coast Artillery veterans may have experienced disappointment at not having had a chance to fire in anger. Nonetheless, their service was honorable and, as solid members of the Greatest Generation, they made an invaluable contribution to homeland defense in anxious times. They earned a lasting debt of gratitude from the Nation and an honored place in history, decreed in our National Anthem:

Oh thus be it ever when freemen shall stand
Between their loved home and war's desolation!

4ᵗʰ Stanza, Star Spangled Banner
Francis Scott Key

Introduction

In May 2004, the US dedicated the World War 2 Memorial on The Mall in Washington, DC, almost 60 years after the conflict's end. Fashioned of granite, bronze and sparkling fountains, the imposing design fits well with the nearby major historical icons of the Nation's Capital. Offering generous illustrative detail, each of the armed services, the Merchant Marine, the states and territories of the time, plus the industrial and home front backbones of the war effort are commemorated in a series of 24 *bas-relief* sculpture panels. The memorial's designers aimed at but missed the completely inclusive recognition of one particular group that stood a front line watch in the most anxious days of the war.

National World War 2 Memorial in Washington

The memorial honors the 16 million men and women who served in the US armed services, the 400,000 who died in the war, and the millions of American civilians who supported the war on the home front. Memorial visitors enter a sunken plaza on ramps which pass by two giant arches representing the two overseas fronts of the war. Even those who served unscathed in those two theaters of war, without hearing a shot fired in anger, sacrificed greatly in defense of democracy and merit the permanent respect of a grateful nation. It is curious, however, that soldiers assigned to the combat front lines in the American Theater are not specifically recognized.

Immediately after Pearl Harbor and the US's reluctant entry into the war as a combatant, there was well-reasoned fear that the US homeland might be attacked and grievously damaged. The Navy and Air Force were unprepared to cope effectively with a foreign invasion or hit-and-run attacks, which might have been attempted along the shores of the Atlantic, Pacific, or Gulf of Mexico. Only the Coast

Artillery Corps of the US Army and the National Guards of some seaboard states stood between a daring enemy and the people, providing the best defensive deterrent they could muster.

At the National World War 2 Memorial, all the long-gone batteries of the Coast Artillery are anonymously lumped-in and remembered only in a general sense, among the total of 16 million who served in uniform during World War 2. But they are not specifically depicted or credited for their front line obedience to orders during the war's darkest hours. Without advocates to urge their recognition, the homeland defense contribution of the Coast Artillery was overlooked by the memorial designers.

In any given month, the journals of veterans' organizations list tens to hundreds of military unit and shipmate reunions as ageing former warriors gather for mutual recognition and remembrance of important service. Coast Artillery batteries seem not to appear in the reunion lists. Perhaps because they didn't fight overseas on the Atlantic or Pacific "fronts," or because they were not called upon to stand and fight-off a seaborne enemy, Coast Artillery veterans are subdued, reluctant to claim their rightful share of history. Modest and unassuming, the coastal cannoneers neither brag nor complain about their duty and their service. Thus, the purpose of this book: objectively telling the story of important defense and deterrent, primarily using the example of the cannoneers at Fort Miles, Delaware.

1

The Pre-Pearl Harbor Strategic World Setting

With wary eyes on Europe and the Far East, Americans prayerfully hope to avoid war...

Contrary to the perceptions of many Americans, World War 2 did not begin with the Japanese attack at Pearl Harbor. To be sure, the formal US *entry* into World War 2 occurred in December 1941 but much of the world had actually been in major, savage combat since the 1930s in Asia, Europe and North Africa. Before the end of 1940, the Japanese had conquered and were bloodying much of the Asian mainland. Beginning in 1939, the Germans had rapidly overrun Poland, much of Western Europe and Scandinavia, and were preparing an invasion of the United Kingdom with an air assault that came to be known as the Battle of Britain. Fascist Italy had conquered and was occupying countries in North Africa. All three Axis powers demonstrated intentions to conquer and consume foreign sources of raw materials.

Overconfident in the imagined protection of great oceans to the east and west, and a mistaken trust that proclaimed neutrality [2] would be respected, even after the Roosevelt administration openly chose sides against the Axis powers, token preparations for effective defense of the US homeland lacked committed resolve. In this fragile pre-war period, the homeland defense perimeter was confined within a set of "frontiers" marked by US territorial waters. Although the inevitability of being pulled into war was a gnawing premonition for many Americans, a replay of World War I history was the imagined script, with US ground troops reluctantly joining allied armies across the ocean, "over there," in Europe. Exemplifying the Nation's general mood, songwriter Irving Berlin rewrote his God Bless America (written many years earlier) in prayerful hope that war would be kept "far across the sea" from the American homeland.

---

[2] President Franklin D. Roosevelt formally proclaimed US neutrality in the war being waged in Europe on September 5, 1939 and again on May 11, 1940.

God Bless America

While the storm clouds gather far across the sea,

Let us swear allegiance to a land that's free.

Let us all be grateful for a land so fair,

As we raise our voices in a solemn prayer.

God Bless America . . . etc."

Underscored by Roosevelt's relentlessly scolding foreign policy, the freezing of Japanese assets in the US, an oil embargo against Japan, and the logistic support given to the enemies of Germany and Italy were interpreted as belligerent acts by all three Axis powers. This Axis interpretation led directly to German attacks against ships of any flag believed to be carrying war materiel from the US to its friends across the Atlantic and led also to Japan's surprise attack at Pearl Harbor.

The strategic importance of the Delaware River and Delaware Bay had been well-understood since World War I. Heavy industries, including shipbuilding, chemicals, steel, and textiles were critically dependent on ports such as Philadelphia, Wilmington, and Trenton. In the early 1940s, much of the crude oil taken to the refineries of New Jersey and Delaware arrived by oceangoing tankers steaming into Delaware Bay. Ships loaded with fuel oil, gasoline and other refined petroleum products then came back down the Delaware River into the bay and out into the ocean to sail along the US east coast to their delivery ports or to join convoys forming to cross the Atlantic. Similarly, vessels carrying military supplies, food, and raw materials were loaded at the Delaware River ports and followed the same routes out into the Atlantic, many to join trans- ocean convoys.

Beginning in 1940, the US watched impotently as submarine wolf packs, homeported in Nazi-occupied France, hunted what Germany deemed legitimate shipping targets bound for the UK and

Russian Arctic ports to assure continued British and Soviet defense of their homelands and their basic survival. As they had done in World War I, Germany included US flag vessels in this target category and several were sunk or unsuccessfully attacked. In 1940-41, the US' feeble anti-submarine defenses were technologically obsolete, small in number, poorly coordinated, and largely ineffective.

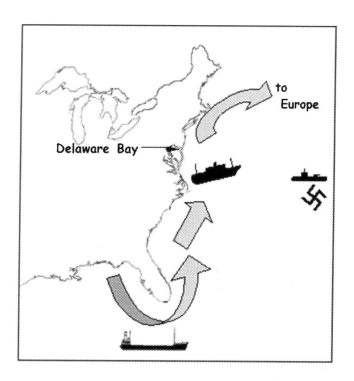

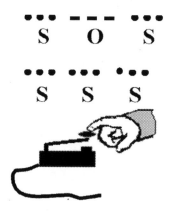

Coastal merchant shipping crews were on 24-hour watch for submarine periscopes. It became so common for the US Navy and Coast Guard to receive "SOS" distress calls, globally in use since 1906, from ships encountering U-Boats that a new, more quickly-keyed distress call "SSS" was coined, specifically meaning "Submarine Sighted." So great was the coastal submarine threat, the Cape May Canal was dug by the Army Corps of Engineers to permit ships to move between Delaware Bay and the Intra-Coastal Seaway along southern New Jersey, thereby avoiding torpedoes from U-Boats prowling the ocean approaches.

The Germans had also deployed armed commerce raiders disguised as cargo ships, which sometimes decoyed unsuspecting freighters and tankers with false distress calls, uncovering their deck guns only when the duped targets were within range. 138 vital cargo ships were sunk by these raiders, which were also especially worrisome to Coast Artillery batteries, lest they be fooled by their clever disguises. American newspaper headlines that sensationalized sinkings just off the east coast caught the attention of many readers, especially those living in Eastern Seaboard states. Some sinkings, accompanied by large explosions and fire, could be seen by American crowds from shore, arousing the same curiosity we feel today when passing the scene of a highway accident.

East Coast beaches were frequently littered with the flotsam of torpedoed ships and occasional corpses. Warrant Officer Ralph H. Trader Jr., serving in the Coast Artillery, remembers the remnants of torpedoed ships washed up on Fort Miles' beach. Still, the offshore waters were as close as the majority expected the war to come and, so long as the routines of American daily life could continue, there was little sense of imminent danger. It wouldn't be until September 1941, as a response to several close-in sinkings, that President Roosevelt issued an "attack-on-sight" order for any German or Italian vessels spotted in US waters.

The German commerce raider Pinguin ("Penguin.") During her 1940-41 operations in the Atlantic and African waters, Pinguin sunk or captured 32 Allied ships before it was itself sunk by the Royal Navy.

The "gathering storm" described by Winston Churchill,[3] sobered only a part of the American Nation. Significant domestic solidarity with Nazi Germany was openly expressed by uniformed, swastika-bannered "Bund" organizations that paraded and filled American big-city sports arenas. Also,

---

[3] Churchill's 1948 post-war analysis

"America First" groups, preaching appeasement and isolation, found outlets in a large percentage of newspapers that echoed their views. Although privately warned of the war dangers by his diplomatic and intelligence advisors, President Roosevelt publicly maintained the reassuring illusion of American isolation with promises to keep war away from the US homeland.[4]

Even as the likelihood of being dragged into war increased to the point that the country's first- ever precautionary peacetime draft was enacted in September 1940, the partisan mood of the Congress was not wholly convinced.[5] The draft was limited to no more than 900,000 conscripts simultaneously on active duty and then only for one-year enlistments. Also that same September, Coast Artillery units of the Delaware National Guard, with four 12-inch guns, were federalized as the 261st Coast Artillery Brigade (HD)[6] at Fort Saulsbury (near Slaughter Beach[7]). The regular Army's 21st Coast Artillery Regiment, organized as two battalions, was stationed well inside Delaware Bay at Fort Dupont. However, both the 21st and the 261st had been in "caretaker" status since the early 1930s, when the likelihood of enemy ships appearing offshore was remote. These units were far from combat-ready.

The Roosevelt Administration's official view was that two wide oceans buffered the US from the rapidly-spreading hostilities abroad and the slumber of coastal defenses was allowed to continue, undisturbed. No Coast Artillery batteries in Delaware maintained an operational watch with guns ready for action in this pre-war period.

Lt. Col. Henry K. Roscoe

In January 1941, elements of the 261st joined the 21st at Fort DuPont, near Delaware City. Henry K. Roscoe, who had been commander of a Delaware National Guard Anti- Aircraft Artillery (AAA) battery was promoted to Major and named to command the 261st. Roscoe advanced rapidly to Lieutenant Colonel when the full 261st was federalized in January 1941. Redesignated a brigade and subordinated to the 21st Coast Artillery Regiment, its

---

[4] Roosevelt's *Arsenal of Democracy* radio address, December 29, 1940

[5] Sobered by the fall of France, Congress passed the Selective Service and Training Act by a single vote, 203-202. The draft was limited to men aged 21-35 and deployments were restricted to the US and territories. The draft age was lowered to 18 in 1942 and the restriction on deployments to foreign soil was lifted.

[6] HD = Harbor Defense

[7] Just inside the mouth of Delaware Bay

headquarters was transferred to Fort Miles in July 1942. The memories of senior US military and federal law enforcement officers, who watched the ominous developments abroad warily, were clear on the breadth of German warfighting methods.

German initiatives included the spectacularly explosive World War I sabotage in July 1916 of over two million pounds of war munitions awaiting export from New York harbor, even though the US was officially neutral.

Military and law enforcement memories were refreshed as late as 1939, when blame for that violent attack, which had killed seven Americans 23 years earlier, was conclusively laid at the feet of Germany. The refresher and its lingering memory served to raise awareness of the threats of sabotage, especially along the coasts and in strategic harbors.

In a military vein, offshore threat assessment was sharply punctuated by the first shots of World War 2 in Europe. Before dawn on September 1, 1939, the war's opening salvoes were fired by the German battleship *Schleswig-Holstein*, which had sailed audaciously into the Polish harbor of Danzig to shell military installations with her heavy main batteries.

September 1, 1939: The battleship Schleswig-Holstein shells Danzig positions.

Also in 1939, an analysis of *Kriegsmarine*[8] gunnery capabilities had revealed that, if war broke out, heavy German ships might be able to shell US coastal assets from positions outside the range of defending Army Coast Artillery guns. The obvious need for longer range guns, brought closer to the ocean shoreline, launched plans to upgrade coastal defenses.

In November of that year, an Army Corps of Engineers survey team from the Fortifications Division in Philadelphia recommended an artillery fort at Cape Henlopen, Delaware, which benefits from the natural protection of the highest coastal dunes between Delaware and the State of Maine. That recommendation became the plan for Corps of Engineers "Project 14," a $22 million[9] development of a Coast Artillery installation on 1155 acres at Cape Henlopen, which are bounded by four miles of Atlantic Ocean beach and a one-mile beach along Delaware Bay.

1941: "Tent City" at Camp Henlopen, later renamed Fort Miles

Project 14 was underway in the summer of 1941 with the White Construction Company of New York as the prime construction contractor. Many of the fort's new concrete facilities were built by subcontractor George & Lynch of Dover, Delaware. But, the mood of the Nation had obviously not

---

[8] German Navy
[9] Approximately 406 million in 2021 dollars

yet shifted to the aggressive "Can Do" spirit that caught on right after the Pearl Harbor attack. In August of 1941, hundreds of Project 14 workmen went on strike for higher wages, which at the time ranged from 90 cents to $1.50 an hour.

Since colonial days, the Cape Henlopen site had been unpopulated and largely unspoiled. Without paved public roads, access over the sand dunes to the ocean was difficult, therefore not a popular beachfront destination for visitors. The Lewes Sand Company had for years collected and marketed beach sand for use in construction projects and had laid its own railroad track right up to the ocean front dunes. A combination of the site's remoteness and those available tracks made it ideal for peacetime training exercises by the Army's 52nd Coast Artillery Regiment based at Sandy Hook, New Jersey.

At the outbreak of the Second World War, the mouth of Delaware Bay was guarded by only two batteries of 155mm guns. Well back from the mouth of the bay, Fort Saulsbury had four 12-inch guns but no capability for sighting enemy targets while they were still out in the ocean. The much-delayed reinforcement of Cape Henlopen did not begin until March 1942 with the backfilling, temporary deployment of four of the 52nd Coast Artillery's 8-inch railway guns on the already-available Lewes Sand Co. tracks. The deployment of our more 8-inch railway guns would wait until September of that year. Nearly three months into a war that was proving extremely difficult for US forces locked in battle with combat-hardened Axis forces, the thinness of the Delaware Bay defenses was worrisome and the threat of penetration by armed naval raiders so credible that in March 1942 an anti-ship boom was stretched across the Delaware River at Reedy Island. The boom was removed in December 1942 as the effectiveness of US Navy and Air Corps in pushing the German fleet eastward boosted confidence.

Uniform insignia of the Delaware Army National Guard

As the fort grew, two major units redeployed to the new site: the 21st Coast Artillery Regiment of the Regular Army and the 261st Coast Artillery Brigade (Harbor Defense) of the Delaware National Guard. At first, the camp (later renamed Fort Miles), had a complement of 24 officers and

21st CAR

8

303 enlisted men living in a rough, tent encampment with communal latrines and hot water only if the sun heated the outdoor pipes.

The fort was, however, manned by over 2500 soldiers housed in wooden barracks by July 1942. Construction was started on eleven observation and fire control towers along the Delaware shoreline from Fort Miles down to just below South Bethany. Concrete for the new towers was mixed with beach sand, which was plentifully available right where it was needed.

Fort Miles was subordinated to Headquarters of the Coast Defenses of the Delaware at nearby Fort DuPont. This headquarters relocated south to Fort Miles in October 1942, with command responsibility for Fort Delaware, Fort DuPont, Fort Saulsbury, and Fort Miles, all in Delaware. Fort Mott and the artillery battery at Cape May Point in New Jersey were also under this command. The 261st Coast Artillery Brigade was one of only two Delaware National Guard units that would retain its original identity throughout the war's duration.

While the mission of Fort Miles was to defend the Delaware Bay approaches to the key industrial and naval facilities on both sides of the Delaware River, the fort provided its own protection with the 198th Coast Artillery (Anti-Aircraft) of the Delaware National Guard and one brigade of the Army's 113th Infantry Regimental Combat Team.

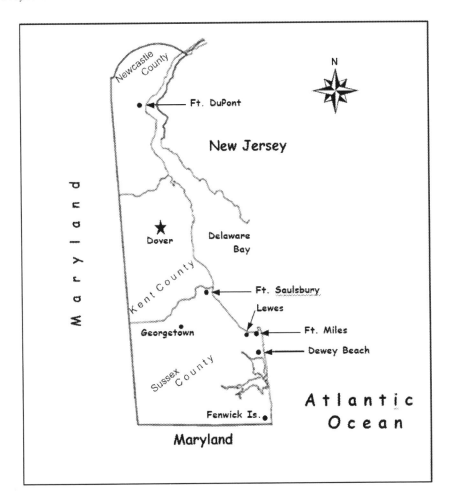

Map 1-1, Delaware: Orientation to principal Coast Artillery locations

2

An Anxious Defense Outlook

December 1941: Was the US about to be invaded?

Americans were at first stunned, then outraged by Japan's infamous surprise attack on Hawaii and, almost immediately, shifted to near panic. Army and Navy recruiting stations were quickly swamped by great numbers of young Americans, ready to enlist and put the Axis aggressors in their place. But the newspapers and movie newsreels of the half-sunken, smoldering Navy hulks at Pearl Harbor and wrecked aircraft at Wheeler Field also inspired a degree of awe at newly-discovered Japanese long-range capabilities.

On the day after the Hawaii raid, it was sensationally but mistakenly reported that Japanese aircraft had overflown Los Angeles. Banner headlines of the December 8th Honolulu *Advertiser*, echoed by mainland papers, blared that saboteurs had landed on Oahu's north shore and the newspaper quoted official Army sources that Japanese paratroopers had also been dropped. Imagined sightings were reported in many places on the west coast and the worst was feared. Naval and Air Force reconnaissance were unprepared to address real offshore threats and it was not known, with any measure of confidence, what to expect next. Invasion was believable and greatly feared.

Badly worsening diplomatic relations with Japan in the autumn of 1941 had led to the calling of several alerts for the US Army and continuing reevaluation of its defense capabilities. The priority of "Project 14," the secret development of Fort Miles as a Coast Artillery installation, already underway, was raised. Ironically, just the day before the Pearl Harbor attack, the War Department in Washington directed the Corps of Engineers by teletype message to make every effort to finish Project 14 with the least delay. The War Department emphasized completing munitions storage and other essential facilities needed for immediate combat operations.

On the evening of December 7th, shortly after the Pearl Harbor attack, a stressed Headquarters, 2nd

Col. Ruhlen

Coast Artillery District in Philadelphia sent a terse teletype message to Colonel George Ruhlen, commanding at Fort Miles: "Condition II Immediately" and then relayed an ominous "Category D" warning message from Washington to be prepared for a major attack. The colonel's staff needed no further direction and sprang into action without delay to start bringing the fort's gun batteries up from Defense Condition III to Condition II. (See Table 2-1).

Defense Condition	Status
I	Maximum unit readiness for combat action. All personnel at battle stations (guns ready to fire, observation towers and radars, projectile and powder bunkers, mine batteries, searchlights, command posts, plotting rooms and communications manned and ready).[10]
II	A state of readiness that could be maintained indefinitely. A selected number of batteries and guns within those batteries plus their combat support were manned and ready. Observation towers, communications and command posts were continuously manned.
III	Minimum readiness. Within the fort, a minimum of one secondary artillery battery and supporting searchlights were manned.

Table 2-1, Coast Artillery Defense Readiness Conditions (1941)

Category	Likelihood of Enemy Attack
A [lowest]	Probably free from attack. Readiness Condition 3 appropriate.
B	May be subjected to minor attacks. Readiness Condition 2 appropriate with preparedness to implement plans for transitioning to Readiness Condition 1.
C	In all probability, subject to minor attacks. Readiness Condition 2 maintained indefinitely with preparedness to go quickly to Readiness Condition 1.
D	May be subjected to major attack. Readiness Condition 2 maintained indefinitely with preparedness to go quickly to Readiness Condition 1. All sections alerted, selected sections augmented, leaves and passes cancelled.
E [highest]	In all probability, would be subjected to major attack. Readiness Condition 1 appropriate, however lowered to Condition 2 when Defense Category E can be reduced to Category D or lower.

Table 2-2, Tactical Defense Categories (1941)

---

[10] Readiness Condition I was usually limited to no longer than six hours

The District Headquarters' "Category D" warning (See Table 2-2) to the batteries at Cape Henlopen was directly tied to the "Condition II" order and caused countless sweaty palms and lumps in young throats as the offshore appearance of an enemy fleet and possibly even landing craft were the reasons they were at battle stations.

Fort Miles and the other Coast Artillery forts across the US were, however, well below full combat strength when President Roosevelt asked the Congress for a "Declaration of War" on December 8th and, even at Condition II, were far from the firepower they would only be able to muster several months in the future, when fully manned and equipped.

Throughout the Nation, in a fog of confusion and frantic reaction, undermanned and untrained military forces were placed at their highest alert levels and Army Coast Artillery batteries were briefed to expect the imminent sighting of enemy warships. Reserve units were activated and hastily deployed, including infantry and artillery units positioned well inland on the Delmarva Peninsula[11] to back-up the Coast Artillery, if enemy landings overran defensive installations such as Fort Miles.

The civilian population was warned of the possibilities of offshore attack and even invasion. At the White House, President Roosevelt speculated on what he would do, if Japanese forces invaded and advanced as far as Chicago and Mrs. Roosevelt urged her daughter Anna to get her grandchildren off the West Coast. The Secret Service practiced timed wheelchair-pushing to the White House basement bomb shelter.

The negligence of earlier defense preparedness loomed large as the Army scrambled to shore-up weakly protected areas with its available, but thinly-stretched units. Headquarters First Army made clear, however, that reserve forces were primarily for defending areas outside the harbor defense installations that were "likely enemy landing areas." Consequently, the coastline extending from Fenwick Island, Delaware south through Ocean City, Maryland lay outside Fort Miles' area of responsibility and, except for otherwise undefined "emergencies," Fort Miles would have to handle

---

[11] Delaware and the parts of Maryland and Virginia lying between Chesapeake Bay and the Atlantic Ocean

its own defense. As commanders of reserve units began responding to mobilization orders with their strength reports, many units were marked with unfilled manpower positions, low supplies of ammunition, and unserviceable weapons, trucks, and other essential equipment.

In particular, coastal defenses in the mid-Atlantic region were basically unprepared and in need of emergency reorganization and resupply. The ocean approaches to Delaware Bay were covered only by two operationally ready 155mm batteries at Fort Miles and one 155mm battery at Cape May, NJ.

Ammunition stocks were low in both locations and fire control posts, communications, and workable procedures were untested and unrehearsed. The only anti-aircraft capability protecting all of the Delaware River harbor defenses was a single battery of four 3-inch guns at Fort Delaware, too far west to provide any protection to the Fort Miles or Cape May batteries.

What if Germany Had Attempted to Penetrate Delaware Bay or Conduct Amphibious Landings from the Atlantic and by Japan from the Pacific?

Although some contemporary dissenting analysts offer interesting opinions, it is believed by many military historians that, in 1941, neither Axis power had seriously planned to invade the United States. However, remembering Germany's brazen battleship attack inside Danzig harbor as the opening act of the September 1939 invasion of Poland, this was certainly not the official view of the Roosevelt Administration or the anxious Army and Navy in December 1941. The first invasion of the Continental US since the War of 1812 was a credible threat and was so reflected in the "Category D" defense condition imposed right after the Pearl Harbor attack[12]. But without a factual historical record, the probable effectiveness of the Coast Artillery in repelling seaborne attacks can only be conjectured. There are, however, instructive examples to consider.

---

[12] See Table 2-2

The Fort Tilden Test

In May 1940, with overwhelmed and exhausted French and British forces retreating toward a final *dénouement* on the beaches at Dunkirk, France, the US Coast Artillery attempted to test fire two old 16-inch guns emplaced on Rockaway Beach at Fort Tilden's Battery Harris for the protection of the approaches to New York City. Those guns had not been fired since 1935 and were not manned by qualified gun crews stationed permanently at Fort Tilden. According to the report filed by Captain Paul Jaccard, the acting Battery Commander, numerous unforeseen problems resulted in a test failure.

Poor visibility prevented simultaneous sightings by the designated fire control stations and the Battery Plotting Room had difficulty in directing the aiming points for a towed target moving offshore in a predictable steady, straight line. The Plotting Room was unable to compute and order a single shot during the target's first transit of the designated field of fire. On the towed target's second pass along the same line, Gun Number 1 was fired but its concussion disabled the timing bell in the Number 2-gun room and that crew had to handle its own timing with a stop watch.

Captain Jaccard wrote in his report, "For ranges up to 30,000 yards [17 miles] the practicability of the 100-foot towers located in the vicinity of Battery Harris is questioned." Those towers, with observation capabilities approximately equal to Fort Miles' towers, were unable to support the Fort Tilden tests with bearings even when the target tug was ordered to come one mile closer to the beach. Captain Jaccard next ordered the two azimuth instruments and crews to relocate to the top of a 200-foot gas tower in nearby Long Beach, NY and to the top of a 200-foot tower supporting the Marine Parkway Bridge, linking Rockaway Beach to Brooklyn.

From the two improvised higher points, usable bearings were obtained and reported for several target transits but out of four shots (two from each 16-inch gun), no hits or near misses were obtained. The gun crews were able to prepare for shots only once every 90 seconds. At the conclusion of the test, copper residue in the barrel of one of the big guns required mechanical removal.

Fort Miles' 12- and 16-inch Gun Tests

Fort Miles' two 12-inch guns were installed in their permanent positions in Battery 519 in August 1943, having been removed from nearby Fort Saulsbury five months earlier. When one of the redeployed 12-inch guns was test fired for the first time, the concussion dislodged and hurled hanging ductwork and loose objects across the gun room into an exhaust vent. Blast overpressure temporarily disabled the gun crew manning positions in the gun room, who were unable to prepare for a second shot. Battery 519 was not operationally ready.

In September 1943, the first test shot from a newly-installed 16-inch gun in Fort Miles' Battery Harris caused major cracks in the reinforced concrete gun room, calling into question the casemate's ability to withstand enemy bombardment. Battery Smith was not operationally ready.

Fort Stevens' Golden Opportunity

As described later in this chapter, a battery of the 18th Coast Artillery Regiment at Fort Stevens, Oregon miscalculated the observed range to a Japanese submarine that was shelling the fort from the Pacific Ocean surface in plain view. Fort Stevens actually did have a shot but held its fire, the Plotting Room mistakenly believing the sub to be out of range.

A Fort Miles Readiness Conclusion

Although the spirit and bravery of the front-line cannoneers is above reproach, the low levels of Coast Artillery training proficiency and the combat readiness of its facilities effectively to engage seaborne invaders suggests that the performance of the gun batteries would have likely been unsuccessful.

For Delaware Bay, the period of greatest invasion danger was from late 1941 (before the Pearl Harbor attack) to the autumn of 1942, when coordinated coastal defense operations by the US Navy and Air Corps had only just started becoming effective. As late as June 1942, German commandos were landed on two East Coast beaches unobserved (see later in this chapter). During the period December 1941 to March 1942, the mouth of the bay was very thinly protected by only eight mobile 155mm guns at Cape Henlopen and four more across the bay at Cape May. The tall observation towers had not yet been built and the cannoneers' views of attacking enemy vessels was no more than eight miles out to sea and then only in daylight and favorable weather. There was no radar and no mines or listening devices had been yet deployed.

Getting to Combat Readiness

On December 10, 1941, three days after the Pearl Harbor attack and two days after the US Declaration of War on Japan, the US First Army started settling down and began businesslike management of Atlantic coastal defenses. It is important to focus on the fact that the US was formally at war only with Japan – not with Germany.

Overall responsibility for coastal defense had long been assigned to the Eastern Defense Command headquartered in New York City. EDC included the 2nd Coast Artillery District in Philadelphia, which was responsible for Delaware River and Bay approaches to the region's industrial and naval assets.

1st Army shoulder patch

Insignia of the 2nd Coast Artillery District

Germany and Italy declared war on the US on December 11th and this district was quickly re-designated by General Order No. 1 as the "New York-Philadelphia Frontier Defense Sector" with two subsectors: one for coastal defense of the Port of New York and the other designated the "Philadelphia Frontier Defense Subsector." Delaware Bay and the Delaware River led inland to the industrial and naval assets of the Philadelphia-Wilmington area. The Coast Artillery mission in this subsector was termed, "Defense of the Delaware." A December 11th order from Eastern Defense Command advised that the Sector Headquarters had been activated and directed the Philadelphia Subsector to:

- Assume Condition Two [13] Standing Operating Procedures with Germany, Italy and Japan designated "hostile."

---

[13] See Table 2-1

- Establish and operate the subsector as preplanned, except that subsector command was delegated to a local Command Post at Fort DuPont.

- Provide "Category B" [14] defense of the subsector against attack by land, sea, and air with support provided by the Navy and Army Air Force.

- Support the Navy in the protection of friendly sea communications and in destruction of enemy forces within your radius of action.

- In cooperation with the Navy, execute underwater harbor defense measures. The Navy was to establish patrols and issue warning to shipping, but mines were to be planted in New York approaches only. Units were ordered to report their progress by messages via wire daily.

- Continue in effect all cooperative measures with the Navy in carrying out their Defense Plan.

A Fearful Time

The Pearl Harbor shock and confusion were followed by months of dismal, confidence-shaking news abroad, prompting many to consult globes and atlases for locating unfamiliar place names in the gloomy bulletins. Three weeks after the Pearl Harbor attack, a long-range submarine of the Japanese 6th Fleet brazenly surfaced off the Big Island of Hawaii and shelled the city of Hilo.

American garrisons were overwhelmed by Japanese forces on Wake Island (December 23, 1941) and Guam (January 10, 1942). British allies surrendered Singapore on the Malay Peninsula in February 1942. US and Philippine forces gave up Corregidor in April 1942. The Japanese invaded and occupied islands of the Aleutian chain west of Alaska in June 1942 and could not be dislodged until March of the next year.

The beginnings of an encroaching encirclement were evident on maps of the Pacific and a fresh round of fear ensued on February 23, 1942 when another Japanese submarine surfaced off California and fired sixteen 5.5-inch shells in a 20-minute period at an oilfield near Santa Barbara.[15] This sub, the I-17, was observed for approximately an hour and twenty minutes on the surface by excited civilians

---

[14] See Table 2-2

[15] Steven Spielberg trivialized the acute National fear and the anxieties of the armed forces in his movie *1941* (Universal/Columbia Films, 1979). This nonsense film also satirizes the February 1942 shelling of the California oilfield by Sub I-17.

on shore. The I-17 was not challenged by the US Navy or Air Force and no Coast Artillery guns were in range to engage the sub. It was last seen sailing calmly away on the surface.

Just two days later, Coast Artillery anti-aircraft batteries fired almost 1500 rounds of anti-aircraft ammunition at what they believed were Japanese planes flying at 9000 to 12,000 feet over the Los Angeles area. An already jittery nation was even further alarmed and confused by the conflicting Navy and Army public releases. The first news, quoting Secretary of the Navy Frank Knox, reported the Navy's conclusion that the gun batteries had responded to a "false alarm" as the Navy concluded that no enemy planes had been over Los Angeles on February 25th.

But the second public release, this time by Secretary of War Henry Stimson, differed sharply from the Navy's view. Relying on Army after-action analysis that up to five enemy aircraft had overflown the area, Stimson was quoted in the newspapers as theorizing that they were either enemy planes operating from secret bases in Mexico or California or that they were light aircraft launched from Japanese submarines offshore. The *Reno Evening Gazette* printed eyewitness reports of at least two waves of bombers, a total of 200 planes, which did drop bombs. Other witnesses, who were quoted in the *Gazette*, thought there was only one wave of planes. One eyewitness said he saw a plane shot down.

The *New York Times* caustically criticized both sides by plainly labeling the Coast Artillery "incompetent," if it mistakenly fired so many rounds at non-existent targets and expressed wonderment at why, if enemy planes had been spotted at only 9000 feet over the city, no Air Corps pursuit planes had gone up to engage them. In context, there was very little to assure worried Americans that their homeland was safe from offshore bombardment, air raids, or even invasion. The situational awareness of Coast Artillery gunners along all three of America's shorelines was sobering with realistic expectations of seeing action against enemy vessels or aircraft at any time.

For the nation as a whole in the first months of 1942, the immediate future was uncertain; the general mood was apprehensive without much bravado. American children practiced "duck and cover" in their classrooms. The forced relocation and internment of Japanese, Germans, and Italians, many of whom were US citizens, was conducted in full public view. On June 21, 1942, the Japanese submarine I-25 surfaced off Fort Stevens, Oregon and opened fire with its 5.5-inch deck gun.

Ironically this was an operational installation armed with old 10-inch guns manned by soldiers of the Regular Army. The fort was hit by 17 rounds. Battery observers could see the sub on the surface firing at them but over-estimated the range and were ordered to hold their fire. After causing only minor damage, I-25 sailed away on the surface.

Along the Atlantic, fishing boats from Lewes, Delaware, which had since colonial times, harvested the ocean off Delaware and New Jersey, were confined to Delaware Bay and local dinner tables had to make do with less-desirable catches of croakers or trout on Friday evenings. In particular, a favorite commercial fishing spot off Point of Capes, close-by Fort Miles, was placed off-limits to all civilian boats.

Citizens' cameras, binoculars, field glasses and other visual aids and signaling devices were prohibited near "restricted" zones. The US Department of Justice requested the Delaware State Police to arrest anyone seen photographing or sketching beach areas. Gasoline was rationed and those, who were able to drive, were required to tape- or paint-over the top halves of their headlights, lest they be spotted by enemy aircraft looking for targets to attack.

Fortunately, Fort Miles' artillery batteries were never called on to repel an attempted penetration of Delaware Bay or to duel with any enemy ships. As the installation was built-up, Fort Miles' impressive firepower capabilities would have been studied by enemy intelligence and likely did serve, to some extent, as a deterrent to enemy offensive action. Except for scheduled target practice and test firings, about which the local townsfolk were alerted so they could open windows that might otherwise be broken by muzzle blasts, Cape Henlopen stayed quiet.

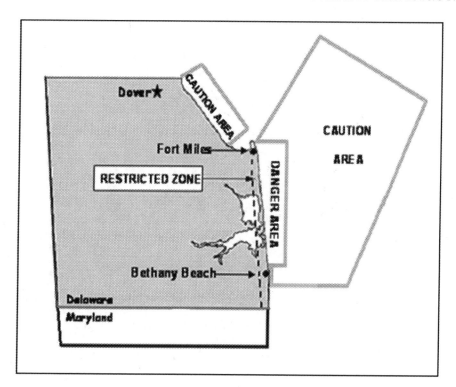

Map 2-1, Area restrictions around Fort Miles

Some of the troops assigned to Fort Miles during the war recalled the duty as "pretty boring" and perhaps, in the later stages of the war, it may have been so. However, a mythical impression, that carried into the post-war years, of a comfortable post by the seashore, where soldiers enjoyed safe, furlough-like duty in a calm atmosphere devoid of frightening excitement, annoyed other Fort Miles veterans, especially those who served in the 1941-42 period. Whatever the relative safety and quiet, they were totally unpredictable qualities and could not have been counted upon. Wartime duty at Fort Miles followed standard Army disciplined procedure and certainly did have its share of tension and scary moments mixed-in with customary garrison boredom.

Very quickly after Japan's Pearl Harbor attack, Germany declared war on the US and, in December 1941, as it had in World War I, deployed submarine "wolfpacks" for three weeks of unrestricted attacks on US and allied shipping. Officially named *"Unternehmen Paukenschlag"* (Operation Drumbeat), five U-Boats, under the command of *Korvettenkapitän* (equivalent to Lieutenant

Korvettenkapitän
Reinhard Hardegen

21

Commander) Reinhard Hardegen, began sinking ships from Cape Cod to Jacksonville, Florida. Hardegen's own sub accounted for nine of the 26 vessels sunk.

At that time, the US was far from effective combat-readiness and Hardegen, nonchalant about the easily-evaded US Navy well into 1942, even impudently surfaced his submarine, U-123, close enough to let his crew come up on deck to see the lights of New York City as surreptitious tourists.

A second wave of U-Boat sorties in the Spring of 1942 sank a further six allied ships along the east coast. During this period of desperate struggle, the Navy, under Chief of Naval Operations, Admiral Ernest King, used its meager Atlantic assets ineffectively to chase reported sub sightings instead of escorting the vulnerable convoys. An exasperated Brigadier General Dwight D. Eisenhower, then a war planner in the office of the Army's Chief of Staff,

Admiral Ernest King

identified Admiral King, as stubbornly obstructionist and wrote [16] in his diary, "One thing that might help win this war is to get someone to shoot King."

The protection of coastal merchant shipping was a very complex challenge needing a level of broad community cooperation that was not immediately available. At the outset of the war, for example, US lighthouses were kept lit and were exploited by U-Boats for navigation along the coast. In another example, coastal electric lighting was a critical but poorly-understood defense problem in the wartime US. Along the ocean shore, suspended particles of salt give the air just enough night-time luminescence to hold the glow of electric light bulbs and conveniently to silhouette ships for a submarine on the hunt.

On the night of April 10, 1942, one of the *Drumbeat* U-Boats' victims was a brand-new tanker. The *SS Gulfamerica*, loaded with 90,000 barrels of fuel oil, was blacked-out, observing radio silence, and zig-zagging her way north past Jacksonville Beach, Florida. Following all the rules, she was nevertheless spotted against the bright lights of a seashore amusement park and torpedoed by *Korvettenkapitän* Hardegen's U-123. Flames from the burning *Gulfamerica* became part of the night's events for shocked amusement park visitors. Thereafter, Florida quickly imposed a state-wide coastal "black-out."

---

[16] March 10, 1942

Delaware started selective "dim-outs" in May 1942 and the front pages of Wilmington and local town newspapers reported the schedules and results of planned fifteen-minute "dim-out" drills. The program was eventually extended to all of Delaware's Sussex and Kent Counties.[17] Quoting military sources, the papers explained "dim-outs" as intended to minimize the silhouetting of vessels without a full lights-off "black-out." In a "dim-out," all electric lights had to be shaded to prevent them being seen from above or from out at sea. Violators were subject to a year of imprisonment and fines up to $5000.00. The program was not, however, immediately successful; Army Major General Phillipson was quoted as reporting the unsatisfactory results of an off-shore inspection from two miles out between the Delaware coastal towns of Lewes and Fenwick Island. Boardwalk and street lights in Rehoboth, near Lewes, were singled out as a serious problem.

Increasingly, information on sinkings plus suspected enemy commerce raider and submarine contacts reported by various vessels and aircraft were assembled by Headquarters of the Eastern Naval District in New York and distributed as "Enemy Action Diaries." These reports were distributed by teletype to military units, such as the 21st Coast Artillery at Fort Miles. Chronicling the numerous actual or imagined contacts with German U-Boats, DF[18] plots on suspected enemy radio transmitters plus unidentified ships and aircraft, the Diaries put pressure on the meager defensive patrol resources available in the form of Navy blimps, Army Air Force and Civil Air Patrol planes and inshore patrol boats. Each incoming report of interest caused some form of Coast Artillery reaction, ranging from simple alert instructions to lookouts in the concrete coastal towers all the way to sending gunners and plotting room staffs to "battle stations," which included readying artillery pieces, powder bags, and projectiles. Although every alert ultimately proved a "false alarm" throughout the war, the anxiety and tension of "this-one- may-be-it" scenarios experienced by all ranks were very real.

To be combat-ready, Fort Miles' Coast Artillery officers and NCOs schooled and drilled the troops of their batteries continuously. Training went on in all weather, night and day, aiming for a smooth operation within self-imposed time limits. Sometimes, young officers deliberately ran gun crew drills with short staffs to force teamwork and cross-training. The Army Field Manuals of the period

[17] It was also in May 1942 that New York City rescheduled night-time baseball games at all three of its Major League ballparks to day games for the duration of World War 2.
[18] DF: Radio Direction Finding

specified that all Coast Artillery officers were expected to be able to perform expertly the duties of every member of his gun crew and that enlisted soldiers were to be instructed in the duties of gun commanders and section leaders, in case they needed to assume those positions. Many of the batteries' guns were emplaced outdoors and their powder and projectiles had to be wheeled by crews pushing hand-trucks from nearby storage magazines. Cold, rain, and wind-blown sand added to the crews' problems and provided plentiful lessons to be learned.

None of the Coast Artillery officers had any illusions about the possibility that an engagement with enemy ships off-shore might be accompanied by return naval gunfire and enemy air attack. The ultimate nightmare scenario, which could not be discounted in the anxious atmosphere of 1941-1942, was an amphibious invasion coming ashore on Delaware beaches.

The *Kriegsmarine* was known to have built at least one aircraft carrier and the capability of warships

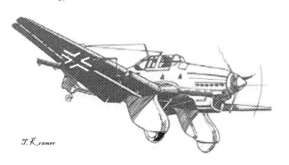

Ju-87 Stuka dive bomber

to catapult seaplanes or lower them over the side was conceded. Later in the war, there even was a fantastic plan, *Unternehmen Pelikan* (Operation Pelican) to deliver two disassembled *Luftwaffe*[19]. Ju-87 *Stuka* dive bombers by submarine to an uninhabited Caribbean island.

Ashore, the *Stukas* were to be reassembled and flown to bomb the Panama Canal locks at Gatun Lake, theoretically denying the strategic canal to the US Navy for months. According to published German accounts, the *Stukas* were already stowed on an underway U-Boat when Berlin believed *Pelikan* had been compromised and it was aborted.

If Berlin had been right, an actual compromise would have provided sensational intelligence information to the US that would have prompted reviews of anti-aircraft defenses at posts such as Fort Miles.[20] In the early days of World War 2, friendly flight plan coordination and aircraft identification

---

[19] German Air Force
[20] Shortly after the February 25, 1942 panic over the mistaken belief that formations of Japanese bombers had overflown Los Angeles.

were very primitive and the sound of overhead aircraft engines brought the "ours- or-theirs" question to many minds, especially at night or during low visibility.

The month of June, 1942, only six months into a war characterized by military reverses and worries about what might be coming next, produced two events that would grab anxious attention at Fort Miles. The first was the sinking of the tug, *John R. Williams*, just off Cape Henlopen, by a German mine. Submarine U-373, one of six the *Kriegsmarine* had specially modified as a mine layer, launched 15 mines, through her torpedo tubes. One of those 15, nine feet long and weighing 2000 pounds, was struck by the tug, which went down with all its crew of 14.

The second, and probably the most jolting event, from a Fort Miles perspective, was the June 1942 front-page news headline that two four-man teams of German saboteurs, comprising *Unternehmen Pastorius* (Operation Pastorius), had been put ashore by submarines off Amagansett, Long Island and near Jacksonville, Florida. Successfully rafting to their destination beaches unobserved during a dark, new moon night, the two teams could have started their destructive sabotage if they had not all been captured, after one of them changed his mind and defected to the FBI. This news, followed by detailed official briefings and exaggerated "scuttlebutt" would have multiplied the usual anxieties of Coast Artillery troops. Tensions among troops stationed along the coast were sharpened by the circulating, embellished rumors of captured U-Boat sailors found to have American movie tickets or grocery receipts in their pockets.

In the midst of all this suspense, former Sergeant Bill Smith, assigned to one of Fort Miles' 3-inch gun crews, remembers an especially stressful July 1942 situation. A US Army Corps of Engineers work-boat was reported by a spotter in one of the towers to be five miles out and approaching the mouth of the bay. High-powered telescope observation of the ship could find no display of signal flags with a prearranged identification code and she was suspected of being an armed German raider in disguise, trying to bluff her way into the bay.

Scope view of inbound freighter displaying signal flags for daily code "M-R-8-8

Maintaining her course, the work-boat did not respond to the fort's repeated attempted radio contacts so two 3-inch warning shots were ordered to be fired across her bow. Smith's battery was ready to fire its next shots for effect when the crew of the suspicious ship at last apparently understood that it was being challenged and quickly hoisted the correct identification flags. To the gun crew's relief, Sergeant Smith's battery was ordered to stand down. That order ended a gut-wrenching episode that continued to intrigue Bill Smith so many years later, when he recalled how close he was to firing at an American ship.

In such an uncertain environment, all the assumed "what-if" possibilities had to be factored-in by the Army's senior planning officers as well as young Fort Miles soldiers on night-time sentry duty, imagining any crashing wave on the beach, any moving tree branch, and any distant muffled voice to be a German commando sneaking up on him with a knife. All sentries had "shoot-to-kill" orders and patrolled with loaded rifles. Tension and watchfulness waxed and waned, ebbed and flowed in direct relationship to full versus dark moons and a month's highest tides that would both conceal and facilitate enemy commando landings.

It is important to note that, throughout the duration of World War 2, the largest portion of the Army stationed within the US was focused on an overseas war. Units were in training, preparing to deploy abroad or were logistically supporting units already overseas. The Coast Artillery batteries stationed along the American coastlines were on the front line and the frame of mind of troops standing watch in Towers #1 and 2, miles south of their post, is particularly worth acknowledging. Especially during black of night, those few men were completely out of friendly visual contact, dependent on fragile communications lines reserved for minimized operational messages, and had only each other for fraternal support.

For the most part, military life at Fort Miles turned out to be a desirable alternative to combat duty abroad but there were enough worrisome moments to go around. In hindsight, we now know that the veterans of Fort Miles were actually safe but, at the time, none of them knew so and their situation might have been very different, if the Battle of the Atlantic had not been decisively won by the Allies. The Coast Artillery's vigilant protection of the nation's harbor approaches must be a gratefully acknowledged chapter of US military history. The troops of the regular Army and National Guard were assigned a critical front line watch along all three coasts and they did their duty.

3

Enemy Threats and Fort Miles Capabilities

Fort Miles primary mission was to defend against Germany's *Kriegsmarine* ...

The hopeful 1930s reliance on the protection of wide oceans contributed to restraining American coast defenses to an anemic, token response to a misunderstood threat. In April 1941, four mobile 155mm guns were towed by trucks to Cape Henlopen and emplaced near the mouth of Delaware Bay. They were joined two months later by four more 155mm guns and an additional four were positioned across the bay at Cape May. At the time of Germany's December 11th Declaration of War on the US, these twelve guns plus a few smaller 3-inchers, all with limited daylight capability, constituted the full Coast Artillery capability for keeping enemy raiders outside Delaware Bay.

The bitter lessons learned and weaknesses exposed first at Pearl Harbor, next during the submarine incident off the California coast, followed shortly by the losses at Guam, Wake Island, and the Aleutians, finally drove late but ambitious plans to fortify the nation's strategic harbor approaches on all three coasts into high gear. Sobering truths, kept secret from the citizenry, tested the confidence of the Roosevelt administration and the most senior levels of the armed forces. Up-to-date resources and enough troops trained to man them using proven tactics had been seriously neglected.

The inability, in 1941-1942, to protect friendly ships just off the Atlantic coast, the brazen submarine shelling of California and Oregon, the panicky confusion during the "Battle of Los Angeles" fiasco plus long lists of worrisome shortfalls everywhere they looked, finally convinced military planners that there was much urgent work to do. The Delaware Bay gateway to key naval and industrial assets was assigned a very high defense priority and the build-up of Fort Miles propelled it ultimately to become the most robustly armed military installation on the Atlantic coast.

But it wasn't until March of 1942 – fully three months into the war - that four 8-inch guns on railway flatcars arrived at Fort Miles and not until six months after that, in September 1942, that an additional four railway guns were emplaced. These guns and their self-contained support cars were manned by the regular Army's 52nd Railway Artillery, which had pre-war experience using existing track from the main line running from the nearby town of Lewes to their firing positions, just behind the beach.[21]

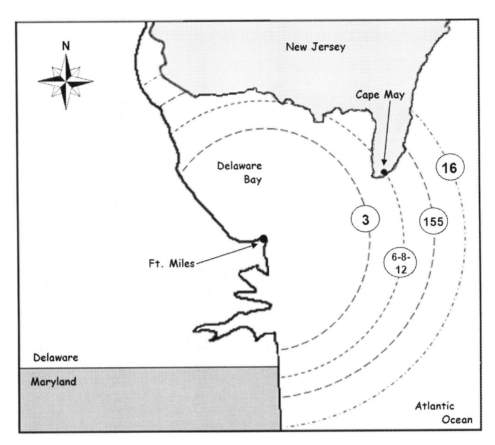

Map 3-2, Maximum ranges of Fort Miles' 40 Coast Artillery guns after September 1943. The map is for general orientation and is not intended as a scale drawing. To simplify readability, the ranges of the 6, 8, and 12-inch guns, which actually were from about 15 to 17 miles, is approximated by the arc labeled "6-8-12." The 155mm guns, with a range of almost 19 miles is approximated by the arc labeled "155." The ~25 mile range of the 16- inch guns is shown by the arc, labeled "16." The ~10 mile range of the 3-inch and 90mm guns, which were intended to engage enemy Motor Torpedo Boats, is shown by the arc labeled "3." See Table 3-1, above, for the actual ranges of all the fort's guns. The guns at Cape May, with a maximum range of approximately 19 miles, could be shown as a circle whose radius reached to Fort Miles and eastward out to sea but is not included here to keep the map uncluttered.

At its wartime height, Fort Miles operated 40 major Coast Artillery pieces in Delaware and Cape May, New Jersey in a wide spectrum of calibers plus anti-aircraft weapons and support systems. These were the Army's largest caliber artillery pieces with varied range capabilities. Many of the guns were

---

[21] The two batteries of the 52nd were redesignated the 287th Coast Artillery in April 1943.

on the ground in open air while others were installed in largely self-contained concrete casemates.[22] Organized into firing batteries, the guns were controlled by command centers and plotting rooms and were supplied from hardened ammunition "igloos" and storerooms.

Later in the war, the fort deployed and controlled extensive underwater minefields and an anti-submarine net across the mouth of the bay between Delaware and New Jersey. Specialists monitored underwater detectors for the sound of approaching engines and propellers. There were powerful searchlights along beach points from Cape Henlopen south to Fenwick Island for spotting ships and aircraft at night.

Primitive radars were installed on steel towers just behind the beach, and the string of surviving concrete Fire Control towers was erected, serving today as prominently visible reminders of wartime dangers confronted. Mixed in amongst all of these weapons and sensors were extensive wire communications, electric power generators and relay stations, and a weather station.

A formerly "Secret" wartime map of Fort Miles is densely crowded with roads, wirelines, railroad tracks, administrative and logistical buildings, barracks, mess halls, and other structures commonly found on major military installations. Many of the more durable structures may still be seen, in various states of repair. Map 3-1 provides a simplified orientation map of the fort, eliminating most features not directly associated with the big guns and observation towers. Completely detailed maps and drawings can be found on various websites and at the Visitor Center at Cape Henlopen State Park.

---

[22] A casemate is a hardened artillery structure, which may be open at its front for protruding artillery pieces. At Fort Miles, the four gun casemates and one mine casemates contained plotting rooms, communications switches, ammunition stores, plus administrative and crew support facilities. Built of reinforced concrete, a casemate's primary purpose in the protection of guns, stores, and cannoneers from enemy bombardment.

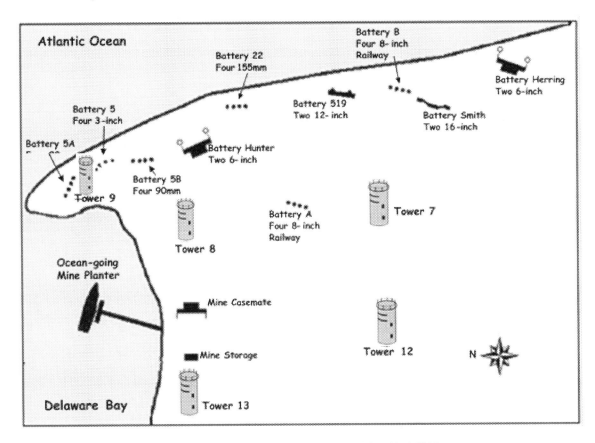

Map 3-1, Orientation to Fort Miles Facilities, 1941-1945

Coastal Cannoneers

At the outset of World War 2, the US Army performed three specific artillery missions with distinctly different classes of artillery weapons.

- The Field Artillery provided direct support to its brother corps (e.g., Infantry, and Armor) and needed to have the mobility necessary to maneuver to positions from which Field Artillery guns could engage what were often, likewise, mobile enemy targets. The Field Artillery's mobility requirement dictated the size and weight of its guns and gave rise to specialized dedicated logistics systems. Field Artillery pieces had wheels, tracks, or were mounted on rail cars pulled by locomotives.

- Anti-Aircraft Artillery (AAA), consisting of heavy machine guns, rapid-fire small-bore artillery, and larger but still small-bore cannon also needed maneuver mobility to protect the units to which they were attached but could also be positioned for point defense. Many AAA assets were deployed in long-term positions with varying levels of defensive fortification.

- Coast Artillery units protected fixed major assets (e.g., cities, harbors, and their facilities) and were based in permanent, defended positions such as forts. Since mobility was not a requirement for Coast Artillery weapons, the size and weight of its guns were not restricted and were typically the largest available. Coast Artillery targets were also expected to have two basic characteristics:

    1. they were expected to be armored combatant vessels and
    2. to have unrestricted mobility that enabled evasive action.

Rationalizing that engaging approaching enemy vessels with heavy, armor-piercing projectiles as far from shore as possible was better than permitting the enemy to approach closer, which would allow the advantage to enemy guns, the Coast Artillery relied on cannons able to throw heavier projectiles over longer ranges. These guns needed no mobility to accomplish their assigned missions and were installed on very stable mounts that helped keep the big guns in place after firing.

This latter consideration was most important; the positions of all the Coast Artillery weapons were very precisely surveyed to enable the application of mathematical triangulation in the targeting process. If the big guns rolled backwards from the recoil of each firing, they would have cost their gun crews precious seconds needed for repointing them and, over time, might have moved well off their carefully-surveyed marks.

Fort Miles assumed responsibility for engaging and destroying a variety of potential threats, within range of its guns, which could materialize in combination, suddenly without warning, day or night, and in any weather. The fort's zone of responsibility was defined by the range of its biggest guns: a circular arc with a radius of approximately 25 statute miles from Cape Henlopen out to sea and up into Delaware Bay. The potential enemy threats were:

- An invasion flotilla of small landing craft heading for the beach, supported by a task force shelling Fort Miles with suppressive fire
- Submarines, submerged or on the surface

31

- Fast motor torpedo boats or destroyers, which might attempt a dash into Delaware Bay, an attack on surface targets in coastal waters, or aim harassment fire at Fort Miles' installations

- Disguised "commerce raiders" that might try to bluff their way into Delaware Bay or shell friendly ships hugging the coast

- Enemy aircraft flying in from over the sea.[23]

Caliber	Projectile Weight (pounds)	Muzzle Velocity (feet per second)	Maximum Range (statute miles)	Sustained Rounds Per Minute**
16-inch	2240	2700	25.5	1
12-inch	1067	2250	14.2	1 to 2
8-inch*	250	2800	17	1 to 2
155mm (6.1-inch)	127	2710	18.7	4
6-inch	90-105	2598	15	4
3-inch/90mm	24	2700	10	5 to 6

Table 3-1, Fort Miles' Firepower

These were eight 8-inch railway guns on railroad flatcars

****Best sustained rate of fire by well-trained and well-practiced crews***

Fort Miles' railway guns were deployed to their emplacements on the batteries' own trains. The railway batteries arrived as self-contained units complete with a rolling plotting room, ammunition storage cars and erectable fifty-foot Base End Stations, which would have provided only an approximately 8-mile view out to sea. The track terminated in eight firing spurs just behind the beach, each spur occupied by an M1A1 railcar mounting a single 8-inch gun. These railway guns were reassigned to other artillery units away from Fort Miles in August 1944.

---

[23] The Army's Coast Artillery Corps was assigned two basic missions: defense against seaborne threats and Anti-Aircraft Artillery (AAA). AAA units far outnumbered the Harbor Defense units and were more widely deployed. Enemy air strikes launched from aircraft carriers or from seaplanes catapulted from ships or put over the side were definite early World War 2 threats. The dedication of the men of the AAA units is gratefully acknowledged, although to keep a narrowed focus, is not detailed here.

Crew of an 8-inch rail-mounted gun fires the piece. In the photo, note the stabilizing outriggers that have been deployed and that the crew has been ordered to face away from the muzzle blast. On the gun platform, the last soldier on the left is holding a sponge on a long stick for swabbing the barrel to extinguish any remaining sparks before the next projectile and powder bags are put in the breech.

Gun Crews – the Cannoneers

Each of the big artillery pieces, such as the 155mm, 6, 8, 12 and 16-inch guns at Fort Miles, needed as many as 30 to 40 crew-members for effective combat.[24] The crews worked under intense pressure having only a few seconds to complete intricate operations while handling heavy, dangerous high explosives and maneuvering an unforgiving metal monster that could easily crush bones that got in the way. Army Field Manuals of the 1940s named and numbered each of the cannoneers and specified their battle station positions with the detail of a football playbook. The "plays" were precisely choreographed for rapid responses to the simple commands shouted out by the officers and sergeants.

Table 3-2, Fort Miles' Changing Order of Battle during World War 2

Period of Operational Service	Emplacement	Number of Guns	Caliber
April 1941 to February 1944	Battery 22	4	155mm (6.1-inch)
December 1941 to February 1944	Battery 26 (Cape May, New Jersey)	4	155mm (6.1-inch)
March 1942 to August 1944	Battery C (Railway flatcar mounted)	4	8-inch
May 1942 to March 1943	Battery 5	4	3-inch /Anti-Motor Torpedo Boat
September 1942 to August 1944	Battery D (Railway flatcar mounted)	4	8-inch

---

[24] Many of the Coast Artillery guns of the 1940s had model variants, could be installed on different mounts that limited barrel elevations, and could fire different projectiles of various weights. Technical details can be found on many websites.

March 1943 to the end of the war	Battery 5A	4	90mm (3.5-inch)/ Anti-Motor Torpedo Boat
	Battery 5B	4	
May 1943 to the end of the war	Battery 7 (Cape May, New Jersey)	4	90mm (3.5-inch)/ Anti-Motor Torpedo Boat
August 1943 to the end of the war	Battery 519 (Casemated)	2	12-inch
September 1943 to the end of the war	Battery Smith (Casemated)	2	16-inch
November 1943 to the end of the war	Battery Hunter	2	6-inch
1944 to the e7nd of the war	Battery 223 (Cape May, New Jersey)	2	6-inch
September 1943 to the end of the war	Battery Herring	2	6-inch
November 1943 to the end of the war	Battery 223 (Cape May, New Jersey)	2	6-inch

Sequences of actions were meticulously planned to avoid crew members getting in each other's way as they worked as fast as they could to complete a step others were waiting to follow. Gun crews rehearsed the sequenced steps of their loading-aiming-firing routines in much the same way as a dance troupe. The Army Field Manuals prescribed a quick operational tempo and the work of Ammunition Squads "at the run" specifying that during operations, "no talking will be permitted" except for necessary orders, instructions, and reports.

It has long been a staple of war movies that depict artillery operations or naval cannon engagements to portray the combined fury of multi-gun batteries by showing numerous muzzle blasts in very rapid succession. An impression is thereby created of imagined capabilities for high rates of fire. However, except for smaller artillery pieces (3-inch/90mm), where a single soldier could load a round and extract the empty brass case by opening the breech, the movies create myth by failing to show the intricate step-by-step teamwork demanded of a big gun crew.

The Army Field Manuals and Training Manuals define the commands, processes, sequences, and contingency actions for the big guns and run to some 50 pages of text and diagrams for each. Space does not permit a tutorial here on the crewing of big artillery pieces but it is appropriate to understand

and acknowledge the disciplined service of all the Coast Artillery cannoneers as an important aspect of the history of a fort and its weapons.

Every big coastal artillery piece was manned by a "Gun Section," composed of a "Chief of Section," a "Gun Squad" and an "Ammunition Squad" plus mechanics from a separate Maintenance Section. The organization described in Table 3-3 uses the Gun Section of a 12-inch piece as a typical example.[25]

Table 3-3, Typical Gun Section

Gun Squad – 25 or more troops	Ammunition Squad – around 20 troops
• Gun Commander • Gun Pointer (traversed the gun left or right) • Chief of Breech (opened and closed it) • Range Setter (elevated and lowered the gun) • Range Display Board Operator • Range Recorder • Azimuth (deflection) Recorder • Some 20 additional Cannoneers, numbered from 1-20 • Maintenance Mechanics	• Chief of Ammunition • 19 additional cannoneers numbered "21" to "38" and divided in two details: – Powder Detail (brought powder bags from the powder magazine to the gun on a wheeled cart) – Projectile Detail (brought projectiles from the projectile magazine to the gun in a 2-man sling, on a wheeled hand-truck, if outdoors, or by ceiling-mounted monorails inside the casemates).

---

[25] War Department Field Manual 4-60, *Service of the 12-inch Gun,* May 15, 1940

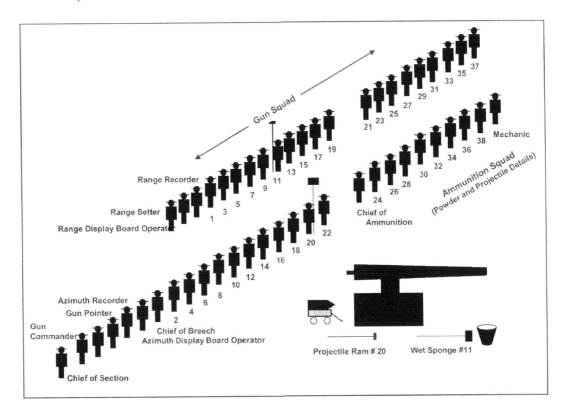

Figure 3-1, Gun Section assembled in formation for inspection. When the Chief of Section is satisfied that all members are present, he commands them to take their assigned battle stations.

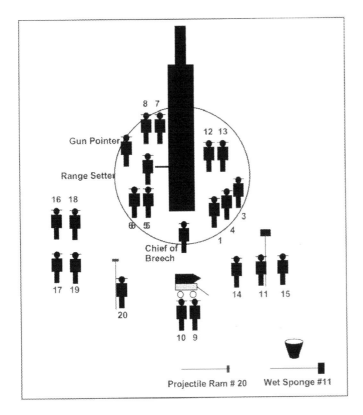

Figure 3-2, 12-inch gun section at operational positions. Only those section members with assigned positions near the gun are shown. Refer to Figure 3-1 for the full gun section.

In another example, the Gun Section of a 6-inch artillery piece consisted of a twelve-man Gun Squad, which was posted with the piece and a twelve-man Ammunition Squad, which moved projectiles and powder from nearby magazines to the breech for loading. 6-inch projectiles weighed between 90 and 105 pounds, too heavy for a single member of the section to safely handle repetitively.

3-inch/90mm ammunition could be handled by a single soldier

Heavier projectiles (here 155mm) were carried by 2-man teams

The typical 6-inch gun used in the 1940s was equipped with a steel shield, four to six inches in thickness, that would have provided limited protection from small arms fire and shrapnel or debris thrown up by nearby enemy artillery impacts. The shield was intended to shelter those of the Gun Squad, who were positioned in close contact with the piece, but provided no protection for those not closely crowded-in or for the soldiers of the Ammunition Squad, who were running back and forth in the open with powder and projectiles.

Wartime photo of one of Battery Smith's two 16-inch guns

At the Fort Miles Museum: restored 16-inch gun from the Battleship Missouri that was swung out over the Japanese Surrender ceremony on September 2, 1945 (right). The restored gun is the center of the three gun forward turret.

A 6-inch shield gun typical of 1940s Coast Artillery installations. This gun is installed on mount set in a circular platform of the type still visible at Font Miles' Hunter and Herring batteries and at Cape May's Battery 223.

Two cannoneers of a Coast Artillery 155mm gun. The Gun Pointer looks though a quadrant sight and points the gun left or right. The Range Setter (in headsets) receives range-to-target data from the plotting room and turns the wheel he is holding to elevate or depress the gun barrel. The desired range of the projectile about to be fired will be determined by the amount of powder loaded with the projectile and the elevation of the gun barrel. 155mm Coast Artillery guns were towed into position by trucks. The guns were not shielded for protection of the crews, who were in the open.

Mines

Anti-ship mines can be designed to float, sometimes tethered to keep them in place on or just below the surface. Their deployment technique is called "mine laying." As the bay was a strategic route for US ships, the use of tethered or free-floating mines could not be used. To protect the Delaware Bay approaches, however, anti-ship mines designed to sit on the ocean floor were also used and their deployment was called "mine planting."

The use of mines to protect the US from seaborne attack has a distinguished history reaching back to the mid-19th Century, when mines were called "torpedoes." During the Civil War attack on Mobile Bay by the US Navy in 1864, Admiral Farragut was actually referring to floating mines in his famous exhortation, "Damn the torpedoes; full speed ahead!" Following the Civil War, mines were the responsibility of the US Torpedo Service, a heritage organization of the Coast Artillery. In his second State of the Union address in 1882, President Chester Alan Arthur included a request for "high-power rifled cannon" for the Torpedo Service, which had not yet been renamed the "Coast Artillery."

During World War I, the Torpedo Service was redesignated the Army Mine Planter Service within the Coast Artillery Corps. Officers of ocean-going mine planter vessels were appointed as the US Army's first Warrant Officers, who wore uniform sleeve insignia similar to the US Navy's.

Uniform sleeve of a 2nd Mate Mine Planter

Cloth Army Mine Planter insignia sewn on uniforms

A "Mine Planter" emblem, slightly different from the standard Coast Artillery emblem, was worn on dress uniform lapels.

These uniform elements were worn throughout World War 2 and up to 1947, when the Mine Planting Service was disestablished. All mines for coastal protection are now within the mission of the US Navy.

In November 1942, the 12th Coast Artillery Mine Planter Battery was transferred from its Ohio River home port at Point Pleasant, West Virginia to Fort Miles, where the battery was resubordinated to the 21st Coast Artillery Regiment as the regiment's second mine battery. The West Virginia cadre was augmented by local Delaware watermen enlistees, who were experienced in crabbing and clamming the waters off Cape Henlopen.

Fort Miles' mine batteries operated from facilities that included mine assembly and storage rooms and two underground explosives magazines. Mine battery troops rolled the heavy mines from their assembly building along rails that led out on a long wooden pier just inside Delaware Bay, where a mine planting vessel such as the *General J.M. Schofield* was moored. These seagoing soldiers loaded the mines aboard the *Schofield* and then planted them (lowered by winches) to the floor of the shipping channel and the ocean bottom, along with their detonator control cables.

Timed mines were programmed to detonate in rapid but very slightly delayed sequences, causing a quick repetition of very powerful sea water shockwaves that would batter an enemy ship below the waterline with greatly multiplied destructive force.

Ocean-going Coast Artillery Mine Planter

24 groups of Type M4 underwater mines of thirteen mines each (total of 312) were planted offshore on the ocean floor and in 11 groups inside the bay. (See Map 3-3). Each of the M4s stood seven feet tall and contained 3000 pounds of high explosives that could be detonated remotely via the underwater cables from a control room ashore in the Mine Casemate. The explosion of multiple 3000 pound mines would create a devastating liquid shock wave that was believed capable of splitting open the heaviest ship hulls sailing on the surface.

Observers high up in Tower #5 were responsible for watching the mouth of the bay and would have reported the approaching progress of enemy vessels while other towers nearer the ocean would have tracked offshore targets. In the mine control room, reported positions were plotted and specific mines would have been set off electrically, just as enemy ships passed above.

The minefields also included both magnetic and timed mines. Six groups of thirteen magnetic mines could be detonated when the steel hull of a passing was detected closely overhead by a magnetic detector loop. At its full strength, the regiment had deployed 455 mines to protect the Delaware Bay approaches.

Quite possibly, Fort Miles' mines would have been the most effective defense against enemy combatants attempting to penetrate Delaware Bay. The exact positions of the planted mines were charted by the Mine Battery and would only have been set off if an enemy ship was plotted just above on the surface. Of course, this would have meant that the enemy ship or ships had successfully come through the big guns' field of fire, possibly firing counter-battery salvoes from their own guns. Assuming that the minefield was not disabled by enemy action and that the Mine Battery with its electrical controls were intact, the minefields represented a formidable last- ditch line of protection.

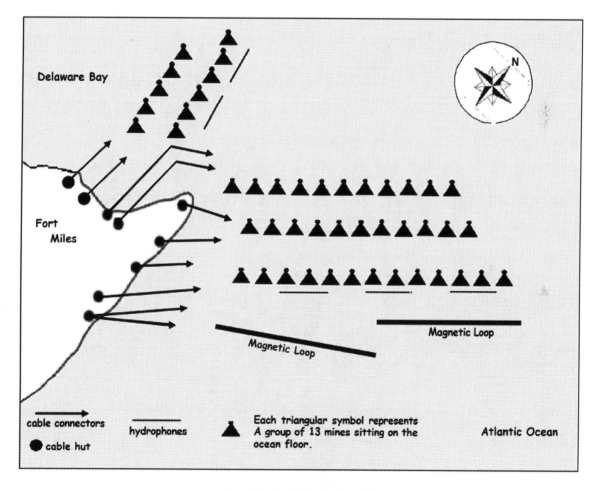

Map 3-3, Fort Miles' minefields

In the 1940s, potential enemy attacks intended to sabotage and disrupt minefields were well-understood. Both surface ships and submarines were capable of dragging grappling hooks that could snag mines, cables and electrical junction boxes, pulling them out of position and possibly snapping control cables. Sound detectors (see below), however, would have recognized the presence of such enemy vessels.

Soldiers of the Fort Miles Mine Battery aboard the General J. M. Schofield planting mines off Cape Henlopen. [Painting by Howard Schroeder; used by permission].

Transiting the Mine Fields

Throughout the duration of World War 2, including periods of highest alert, friendly ships continued to require passage into and out of Delaware Bay. A Harbor Entrance Control Post (HECP), jointly manned by the 21st Coast Artillery and the Navy, was established in Tower #10 at Fort Miles. The HECP maintained SCR-582 radar and voice radio contact with all friendly ships coming and going. The captains of all vessels were directed by the Navy and Coast Guard to await clearance by the Cape Henlopen HECP before entering or exiting the bay.

Ships were visually identified and granted clearance based on pre-arranged challenges and responses that used simple voice passwords, blinking lights, and code letters hoisted in signal flags. When the HECP granted clearance, the 21st Coast Artillery was advised. Spotters high up in the towers kept an eye on transiting vessels to stay alert and to practice their tracking and plotting skills.

The main shipping channels were marked out with buoys and ships, with professional pilots on board, cautiously sailed over the planted mines. At the outset of the war, all pilot boats nationwide were "drafted" as reserve vessels by the US Coast Guard and many members of the Pilots Association of the Bay and River Delaware joined the Coast Guard for the duration of the war.

Pilot Walter Bennet, who enlisted in the Coast Guard and finished the war as a Lieutenant Commander, recalls being unafraid of crossing and recrossing over the minefields. He was aware of great secrecy about Fort Miles' operations but knew that Mine Battery observers always had his vessel in their scopes. Bennet's trust was borne out: no accidental mine firings caused any damage to friendly vessels handled by the professionals of the Pilots Association.

***Control panels located in the Ft. Miles Mine
Casemate for remotely detonating mines.***

Radars

The Army Signal Corps took the first steps toward modernizing support for coastal defenses as early as 1937. A requisition for new operational capabilities specified off-shore ship tracking with measurement of azimuth and range (distance) for use in coast artillery gun laying. Radar and infra-red showed early promise, both technologies being in their infancies, but by 1938, radar was showing better promise and a prototype was ordered. Nevertheless, with wary eyes on the combat use of bomber aircraft by the Germans in the Spanish Civil War and by the Japanese in China, air defense research was prioritized and development of the coast defense radar project progressed very slowly by comparison.

It was the alarming reality of U-Boat and commerce raider attacks on allied shipping just off the US east coast that finally drove the reenergizing of coast defense preparations, including an accelerated development of radar. The US quickly absorbed radar experience shared by the British with the Signal Corps and the Radiation Laboratory of the Massachusetts Institute of Technology. An operational capability was shortly realized with successful trials of a medium wave radar developed by MIT and put into production as Signal Corps Radio Model 296 (SCR-296).

The SCR-296 had a six-foot by six-foot antenna array, steerable by one of the five soldiers assigned to crew the radar. This "Azimuth Operator" slowly turned the antenna horizontally with a remotely-controlled electrical servo-motor. The azimuth, expressed as the number of degrees of magnetic compass bearing, was telephoned to the battery's plotting room by an "Azimuth Reader," peering under a small hood at a radar scope that was so small and dim, compared to later models, that the readers and operators switched places about every half hour to avoid eye strain. Two "operators" and two "readers" worked in small buildings adjacent to the radar tower. A technician monitored the 2.5 kilowatt electrical power generators and rounded out the crew of five.

Unlike later radars that would join the Army's inventory, bringing 360-degree continuous sweeps, the SCR-296 was manually "pointed" by the Azimuth Operator and emitted pulses of radio energy in a stationary narrow beam where it was pointing till the antenna was re-pointed in a new direction. This was a major technological limitation; rather than serving as a principal search resource, repeatedly sweeping the ocean approaches out to the horizon, the SCR-296 depended on an observer in one of the fire control towers visually spotting a potential target and advising the radar operators where to point the antenna. When occasionally used in a broad search mode, the Azimuth Operator very slowly slewed the antenna, looking for a reflected target in the beam displayed on the radar scope. If the slew was too fast and the operator was unable to halt the slewing motion quickly enough, the antenna had to be turned back in the opposite direction, in the hope of relocating what was a moving target on an unknown course. This radar had no height finding capability.

Also, once the radar had acquired a target vessel, the Azimuth Operator had to keep the antenna pointed at the underway target by slewing the antenna. To closely coordinate the radar and visual sightings, the SCR-296 radar antennas were set up directly behind and higher than the concrete observation towers. This assured that the azimuths obtained by radars and soldiers using optical instruments, such as telescopes, would be the same. Although the frame towers that supported the radars are now gone, their concrete footings remain and can be seen at some of the fire control tower locations.

The SCR-296 had a nominal operational range of 45 miles; however, this was really a maximum line-of-sight capability made possible only by basing its antenna on a very high hill or tall structure.

According to its operations manual, the SCR-296 had a dependable range of only 11.4 miles on a destroyer-sized target when employed at a height of 145 feet, which was approximately double the height of the tallest concrete fire control towers. The manual recommended that the radar should be mounted not less than 100 feet above sea level, with 150 to 500 feet the optimum range.[26]

The "view-to-horizon" formula, explained in Chapter 4, for visual observation applies equally here. The radar set's range was, therefore, limited by the height above sea level of its antenna, actually not adding to a battery's visible range.[27] Weighing-in at just under fifty tons, the SCR-296 and its associated support equipment was too heavy and bulky for mobile operations.

On balance, the SCR-296's performance could only be judged "marginal." In addition to its low surveillance capability, this early radar provided return resolution and azimuth discrimination too imprecise to separate multiple targets closer together than 275 yards and within twelve degrees of azimuth. The set was unreliable for accurately tracking moving targets and for fixing miss-splashes.

Working with his counterpart "Range Reader," the "Range Operator" turned a knob that kept the radar pointed at the target. A vessel out at sea would be displayed on the radar scope, the "Range Reader" noted the range indicated on the adjustment knob and telephoned the measured target range to the Plotting Room, where it was used with visually-acquired azimuth and other range data the plotters had received.

Roma Saltzgiver, a Coast Artillery radar officer, who served on SCR-296s during the 1940s, recalls the set's ability to track practice projectiles shot from his battery's guns all the way out to their impacts in the ocean and to accurately measure the range they were hitting but the radar had been pre-set for a known azimuth.

Although the radars were most critically needed in the 1941-42 early years of the war, they were not available for operational service until November 1943, when Fort Miles' status had already been

---

[26] The actual installed heights of Fort Miles' SCR-296 radars is a subject for continuing research.

[27] A formerly "Secret" map of Fort Miles depicts SCR-296 radar coverage as a set of overlapping arcs with a 25-mile radius stretching along the coast from Cape Henlopen down to the location of Fire Control Tower #1, just south of the town of South Bethany. This map also shows the coverage provided by the SCR-296s at Cape May, New Jersey for the mouth of Delaware Bay.

relaxed to Defense Category B.[28] A total of six SCR-296 radars was installed between Bethany Beach and Cape Henlopen. A seventh was positioned across the bay at Cape May, New Jersey to support the 6-inch and 155mm batteries there.

Five of the radars were designated as primary targeting support for individual gun batteries but all of them could function as a secondary resource for any of the other batteries. Although they were never needed to direct fire at a hostile target, the SCR-296s consistently contributed to tracking and ranging practice targets when nighttime conditions made visual tracking unreliable. Coast Artillery doctrine, set down in Colonel C.C. Hearn's textbook years earlier in 1907, suggested that ". . .naval attacks against coast fortifications will seldom be conducted in broad daylight."[29]

In an era predating night-vision equipment, spotters with binoculars or telescopes were unlikely to see a blacked-out ship on a dark night and were at a distinct disadvantage when rain or fog reduced visibility, even when the searchlights were turned on. Under normal conditions, daytime visibility from Fort Miles' gun positions was approximately 8.5 miles at best.

Capabilities were improved with the late-1943 advent of better gun laying radars. However, early sets, such as the SCR-296s were nominally capable of detecting a ship mile out to sea on the blackest night but provided poor discrimination of targets close together and could not distinguish friend from foe.

This shortcoming meant SCR-296s could not have been relied upon as a single source for a fire mission, if both friendly and enemy ships were mixed in a fluid tactical engagement. The objective was to permit the soldier acting as plotter to estimate the enemy target's course, mentally calculating a projected path some minutes ahead.

The troops practiced and were disciplined to concentrate on the field of fire allocated to their own battery. In this way, if a number of enemy targets could be seen, spotters in a tower supporting an 8-inch battery would be focused on ships approaching or already in an arc with a 12-mile radius from the 8 inch guns. In the best scenarios, radar and visual observation complemented and confirmed

---

[28] At Defense Category B, an enemy invasion is considered unlikely. (See Tables 2-1 and 2-2 for descriptions of Defense Categories and related Defense Readiness Conditions).

[29] C.C. Hearn, US Signal School, *Fire Control and Direction for Coast Artillery,* 1907

each other, although the SCR-296 could usually be expected consistently to track targets out to the horizon, once they had been acquired, while troops in the towers could not, if they were unable to see.

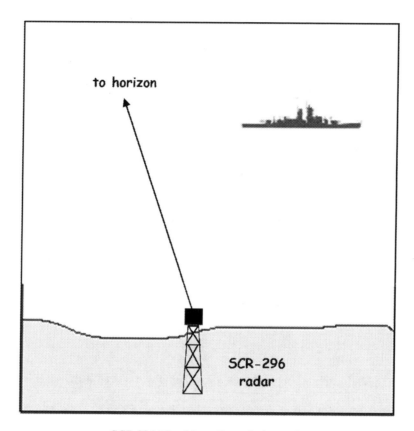

SCR-296 "fixed beam" gun laying radar

It must also be acknowledged that Germany demonstrated effective Electronic Countermeasures (ECM) against British air defense radar very early in the war during the Battle of Britain (1940). It may be surmised that the Germans had a Radar Order of Battle cataloging the precise locations and operating parameters of Fort Miles' SCR-296s beginning shortly after their being placed in service in November 1943. The *Kriegsmarine* would probably have included some ECM techniques, such as dispensing chaff or electronic jamming, as part of an attempted dash into Delaware Bay. In the early 1940s, techniques for overcoming ECM were generally not available and the Coast Artillery and Signal Corps, fully aware of RAF experiences in the Battle of Britain, would have expected their radars to be seriously degraded in a determined German penetration attempt. But Fort Miles' radar capabilities only became operational after the German threat had been pushed substantially eastward, away from the US shoreline.

SCR-582 Radar

In addition to the SCR-296 gun-laying radars, an SCR-582 harbor surveillance radar was installed atop one of the tallest of Fort Miles' concrete towers. The SCR-582 antenna was mounted on a 31-foot steel framework on the roof of 95-foot tall Tower #12, situated near the Harbor Defense Control Post, which was in Tower #10. This radar antenna, at an elevation of 126 feet, could scan the ocean approaches and parts of Delaware Bay out to a horizon just over 15 statute miles out.

Searchlights

Large searchlights, five feet in diameter, were deployed in pairs along the Delaware beachfront from Cape Henlopen to Fenwick Island and in New Jersey from Cape May Point to Wildwood. (See Map 3-3, below and, in Annex B, an official 1945 map showing the New Jersey searchlight locations). In keeping with the standard vocabulary of the Coast Artillery Corps, the pairs were designated "Searchlight Batteries."

The very powerful lights, some on raised wooden platforms and some on the sand, were positioned to illuminate suspicious vessels out at sea for the troops in the towers to check with optical instruments. Searchlights could also be pointed skyward, searching for aircraft overhead, that would be targeted by the fort's AAA crews. As shown by the map in Annex B, the entire protected shoreline was completely overlapped to guard against enemy landing parties paddling to the beach unobserved.

The lights were estimated to be visible from 200 miles away, which was not relevant when considering vessels closer than a 14-mile horizon but did suggest good capability against aircraft at high altitudes. Each individual searchlight was supported by its own gasoline-burning 25 kilowatt electric power generator.

The output of each searchlight was one million candlepower produced by electrical "arcing" between burning pairs of carbon rods. The rods burned at 3000 degrees Fahrenheit and had to be replaced after only two hours of use.

Searchlights were most effective in clear air and at shorter distances. Fog or rain significantly reduced their usefulness as the lights merely illuminated and exaggerated moisture in the air. As early as 1907, then Captain Clint Hearn of the Army Signal School warned that searchlights were "without value" at dusk or dawn "for this same reason and to be sure that searchlight beams were not permitted to touch the ocean's surface."[30]

The lights' brightness diminished as target distances increased and really provided effective illumination for only approximately 4.5 to 5 miles. Perhaps the lights' greatest liability was their own visibility to enemy naval or air forces, which could use the fixed positions of the lights as points for aiming suppressive fire.

Coast Artillery Searchlight battery at Fort Miles.

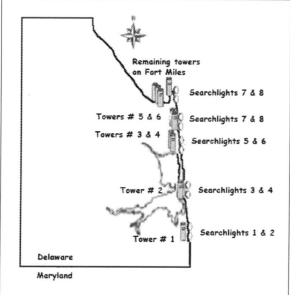

Map 3-3, Searchlight deployment along the Delaware coast.

---

[30] Hearn, *ibid*

William C. Grayson

Anti-Submarine Net and Sound Detectors

During the 1940s, the upper reaches of Delaware Bay were believed too shallow[31] for submerged U-Boat navigation from the ocean all the way to the area's major industrial port cities on the Delaware River. However, nighttime penetration of the mouth of the bay by a U-Boat that might surface well inside the bay, was considered a real threat and the US Navy stretched an anti- submarine net equipped with underwater listening devices across the bay. An in-place net would have forced a U-Boat captain to attempt to slip into the bay on the surface at night, when a black submarine with a low-observable profile would be difficult to spot. The listening devices were counted on to reveal propeller noises, which would have prompted the use of searchlights followed by artillery fire and the remote detonation of underwater mines. No U-Boats were known to have attempted entering the mouth of Delaware Bay as U-123 did off New York City in December 1941.

Fort Miles' Warfighting Towers, Gun Emplacements and Other Surviving Structures

Fort Miles' towers were constructed and specifically positioned to provide unobstructed and extended observation of those areas of the Atlantic Ocean and Delaware Bay assigned for its defense. Sixteen towers were built during World War 2; twelve in Delaware and four across the bay: two at Cape May and another two in Wildwood, New Jersey. When the towers would have been most critically needed – from late 1941 through the autumn of 1942 – they existed only as planned construction. Although they were probably placed in service somewhat earlier, the towers were not accepted by the Army until May 1944. That was quite late in the Battle of the Atlantic and US confidence, borne of having pushed the German threat far from American shores, had already permitted a relaxation of Coast Artillery combat readiness.

Of those towers remaining in Delaware[32], five are within the former Fort Miles perimeter and six are spaced along the ocean beach running south toward Delaware's border with Maryland.

---

[31] Less than 40 feet
[32] One tower, formerly designated "Tower 10," has been demolished.

All of the towers share some common characteristics; however, none are exactly identical. In the tense early days after the US' entry into World War 2, the towers were urgently required. For expediency, beach sand available in unlimited quantity just where it was needed, was used in the concrete mix even though the Corps of Engineers assumed that would shorten the towers' lives to approximately twenty years. In fact, all thirteen of the surviving towers are now approaching 80 years of age with none currently showing signs of dangerous decay.

The thirteen are appropriately referred to as "observation" or "fire control towers." When equipped with optical instruments, such as azimuth telescopes for obtaining bearings on target vessels at sea or in Delaware Bay, the towers are referred to as "Base End Stations," as has been discussed earlier. A telescope that brings a distant image ten or twenty times "closer" also magnifies movement or vibration of the telescope or its supporting platform on the same scale. As "jitter" would have degraded observed images, very solid, steady platforms were needed for the optical instruments and the towers' common design accommodates that need. All are made of reinforced concrete, are seventeen feet in diameter, and sit on foundations of heavy creosoted beams buried deep in the sand to minimize vibrations. The towers' cylindrical form was intended to present a streamlined aerodynamic shape, minimally affected by wind loading, which would cause disruptive vibration. The basic design included interior concrete floors with circular holes for ladder access and concrete disc roofs slightly bigger in diameter than the seventeen-foot tower walls. Telephone cables, which were critical for reporting observed azimuths, entered the towers' bases through metal conduits located at the rear, facing away from the ocean. This latter choice was intended to use the tower itself to shield the cables from destruction by enemy bombardment.

Metal conduits protruding from the base of Tower #5 on a side facing away from the ocean. These conduits originally exited the tower well below the sand but have now been exposed by the constant surf, which has eroded the tower's site on the beach

All of the remaining thirteen towers have observation slits in the upper reaches of the tower structure running 120° or one-third of the way around the circumference. The slits gave the optical instruments as well as artillery observers with binoculars a view toward the assigned target area for the fort's guns. The towers do not, however, show a common design with respect to the number or grouping of the slits.

This characteristic is explained and illustrated below. Curiously, although their principal purpose was to obtain a longer-range view though increased elevation, most of the towers are of different heights. The number, shape, and placement of windows also differentiates the towers. See the illustrations below.

The Delaware Towers

Tower # 1

Location: On Delaware Route 1 in Fenwick Island, just south of Logan St, South Bethany. 38-30-35N, 75- 03-26W.

Base Height Above Sea Level: 12 feet.

Total Tower Height Above Sea Level: Tower height just over 37 feet; total height 49 feet above sea level (upper observation slit at 45 feet above sea level).

Maximum View to Horizon: 8.2 statute miles.

Capabilities and Purpose: Southernmost of the Delaware Bay defenses, approximately five miles south of Tower #2 and fifteen miles south of the main Fort Miles complex. With four azimuth-measuring instruments, Tower #1 was an observation tower for 16-inch Battery Smith and 12-inch Battery 519 (both about 20 miles to the north). Tower #1 provided a view 8.2 miles southward along the coast to cover the full 25-mile range of Battery Smith's 16-inch guns out to an 8.2-mile horizon. Searchlights 1 and 2 were at the Tower #1 location.

Tower # 2

Location: On Delaware Route 1, 1.3 miles south of the Indian River Inlet Bridge. Situated between buildings of the Atlantic Watergate and Indian Harbor Village developments. 38-35-41N, 75-03-69W.

Height Above Sea Level: 9 feet

Total Tower Height Above Sea Level: Tower height 45½ feet; total height 54½ feet above sea level. Four observation slits at approximately 37 and 46 feet above sea level.

Maximum View to Horizon: 9 statute miles

Capabilities and Purpose: With eight azimuth-measuring instruments, Tower #2 provided observation support for:
• 16-inch Battery Smith (2 guns)
• 12-inch Battery 519 (2 guns)
• 6-inch Battery Hunter (2 guns)
• 6-inch Battery Herring (2 guns)

Tower #2 provided an extended view 9 miles southward along the coast to cover nine miles more of the range of Fort Miles' guns than was visible over the horizon seen from the fort. Tower #2 housed a fire control switchboard. An SCR-296 radar antenna stood immediately behind Tower #2; the antenna's concrete footings are still visible on the ground. Searchlights 3 and 4 were at the Tower #2 location.

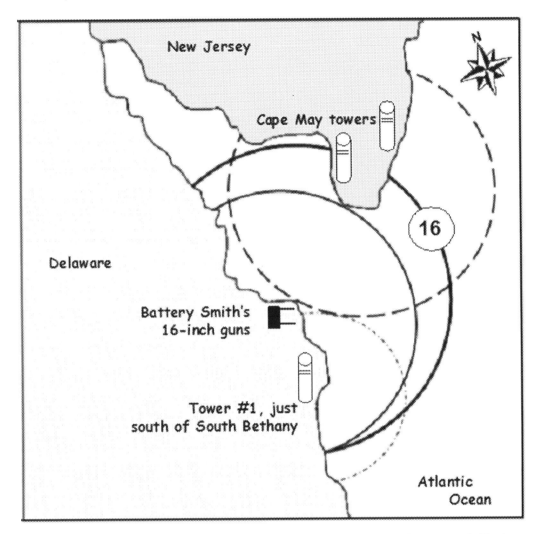

Map 3-4. Tower #1 (Fenwick Is.) and the towers at Cape May provided observation to extended horizons for Battery Smith's 16-inch guns. Although the maximum range of the 16-inch guns was 25 miles, none of Fort Miles' fire control towers had a view of a 25-mile horizon. The bold circular arc represents Battery Smith's 25-mile range. The smaller enclosed arc marks Fort Miles' 14-mile maximum view. The dashed-line arcs represent Tower #1's 8.2-mile view and the Cape May towers' 11.4-mile view. A significant "blind spot" remained for the 16-inch battery.

Tower # 3	
Location: On Delaware Rt. 1, in Delaware State Seashore Park at Tower Road. 38-04-28N, 75-04-28W. There is an informative marker in the parking lot.	
Base Height Above Sea Level: 8 feet	
Total Tower Height Above Sea Level: Tower height 57 feet; total height 65 feet above sea level. Two observation slits at 49 and 57 feet above sea level.	
Maximum View to Horizon: 10.8 statute miles	
Capabilities and Purpose: With four azimuth-measuring instruments, Tower #3 was the southern Base End Station for 6-in Batteries Hunter and Herring. Tower #3 is paired with Tower #4, separated by exactly 900 feet – a presurveyed baseline. SCR-296 radar antennas stood immediately behind Tower #3; the concrete footings of two radar antennas are still visible on the ground.	

Tower 3 Restoration: Beginning in 2008, Tower 3 was undergoing restoration in a project partnered by the Delaware Seashore Preservation Foundation and the Fort Miles Historical Association. When restored, the tower is planned to house a circular staircase that visitors will be able to climb.

Tower #4

Location: On Delaware Rt. 1, in Delaware State Seashore Park at Tower Road. 38-04-32N, 75-04-28W.

Base Height Above Sea Level: 8 feet

Total Tower Height Above Sea Level: Tower height 56 feet; total height 64 feet above sea level. Two observation slits at 47 and 55 feet above sea level.

Maximum View to Horizon: 10.7 statute miles.

Capabilities and Purpose: With four azimuth-measuring instruments on two observation levels, Tower #4 was the northern Base End Station for 6-in Batteries Hunter and Herring (paired with Tower #3, separated by a baseline of exactly 900 feet). Searchlights 5 and 6 were located with Towers #3 and 4.

Tower #5

Location: On the beach opposite Gordon's Pond in Henlopen State Park. 38-44-81N, 75-04-86W.
Base Height Above Sea Level: 1 foot (2004 GPS measurement; probably significantly lower than during the 1940s but unknown).
Total Tower Height Above Sea Level: Tower height 47 feet; total 2004 height 48 feet above sea level. Two observation slits at 31 and 39 feet above sea level.
Maximum View to Horizon: 9.2 statute miles
Capabilities and Purpose: With four azimuth-measuring instruments on two observation levels, Tower #5 was the Southern Base End Station for 12- inch Battery 519 and the underwater Mine Battalion.

Tower #6

Location: On the beach opposite Gordon's Pond in Henlopen State Park. 38-44-96N, 75-04-87W.
Base Height Above Sea Level: 1 foot (2004 GPS measurement; probably lower than 1940s but unknown).
Total Tower Height Above Sea Level: Tower height 64 feet; total 2004 height 65 feet above sea level. Two observation slits at 31 and 39 feet above sea level.
Maximum View to Horizon: 10.7 statute miles.
Capabilities and Purpose: Tower #6 is paired with Tower #5, separated by exactly 900 feet – a presurveyed baseline. Tower #6 was the northern Base End Station with a total of six azimuth-measuring instruments on three observation levels: one each for 6-inch batteries Herring, Hunter and Smith. Searchlights 7 and 8 were at location of the Towers #3 and 4.

Tower # 7
Location: In Henlopen State Park, 38-46-58N, 75-05-57W.
Base Height Above Sea Level: 40 feet.
Total Tower Height Above Sea Level: 110 feet.
Maximum View to Horizon: 14.1 statute miles.
Capabilities and Purpose: Just behind 12-inch Battery 519 and very close to former 8-inch Railway Batteries A and B. Tower #7 had azimuth-measuring instruments on three levels, each with an observation slit, and housed observers reporting to controllers in the Mine Casemate. This tower is open to the public and may be climbed to its roof. Visit website http://www. destateparks.com/chsp/ chsp.htm; this website offers a 360 degree panoramic view from the top of Tower #7, illustrating a clear-day view to a horizon just over 14 miles out to sea and across Delaware Bay toward New Jersey.

Approximately 14-mile view from the upper observation slit of Fort Miles' Tower # 7

__Interior of Tower # 7.__
__The vertical window__
__openings had glass__
__installed when the tower__
__was in operational use__

Tower # 8

Location: In Cape Henlopen State Park.

Base Height Above Sea Level: 33 feet.

Total Tower Height Above Sea Level: Tower height 73 feet; 106 total feet above sea level. Two observation slits at 93 and 102 feet above sea level.

Maximum View to Horizon: 13.8 statute miles.

Capabilities and Purpose: Base end and spotting stations for 16- inch Battery Smith and 12-inch Battery 519. Very near 8-inch Railway Batteries A and B. Tower #8 is located about a third of a mile due west of Battery Hunter. Searchlights #9 and 10 provided illumination for spotters in this tower.

Tower # 9

Location: In Cape Henlopen State Park and currently forms the columnar foundation of the Delaware River and Bay Pilots' Ship Reporting Station, which sits atop. 38-47-66N; 75-05-50W.

Base Height Above Sea Level: 22 feet

Total Tower Height Above Sea Level: 1940s height 24.5 feet; 42.5 total feet above sea level.

Maximum View to Horizon: 6.5 statute miles

Capabilities and Purpose: Tower #9 had three observation slits and provided support to 6-inch batteries Herring and Hunter, the Mine Battery, and anti-Motor Torpedo Boat guns emplaced near the northern tip of Cape Henlopen.

Left: Displayed in Cape Henlopen State Park, a 3-inch gun of the type assigned to Anti-Motor Torpedo Boat Battery B and Below Right: 3-inch brass shell casing containing the explosive powder that drove the attached projectile forward. The shell's self-contained powder and projectile combination was light enough to be lifted and inserted in the gun's breech by a single cannoneer, permitting a high rate of fire. Below Left: in 1943, shielded 90mm guns replaced the 3-inch guns, considered less reliable.

Tower # 12	
Location: In Cape Henlopen State Park, 38-46-54N; 75-06-04W.	
Base Height Above Sea Level: 30 feet Tower height 65 feet; 95 total feet above sea level. Two observation slits at 73 and 81 feet above sea level.	
Total Tower Height Above Sea Level: 95 feet	
Maximum View to Horizon: 13.1 statute miles	
Capabilities and Purpose: Harbor Defense Observation Post and Searchlight Control. Later topped by a model SCR-582 surveillance radar.	

Tower # 13	
Location: In Lewes on US Route 9, immediately opposite the Lewes-Cape May Ferry terminal. 38-46-81N, 75-07-20W.	
Base Height Above Sea Level: 9 feet	
Total Tower Height Above Sea Level: Tower height 81 feet; 90 total feet above sea level. Observation slits at 73 and 81 feet above sea level.	
Maximum View to Horizon: 12.7 statute miles.	

Capabilities and Purpose: Base end station for 6-inch batteries Herring and Hunter. This tower has two observation slits for a total of four azimuth measuring instruments. Located on shore of Delaware Bay. Tower 13's views were concentrated on the bay from its mouth immediately to the south and north to a horizon of 12.7 miles.

Battery Smith Casemate	
Base Height Above Sea Level: 27 feet.	
Total Height Above Sea Level: The casemate is buried as it was during WWII but is now overgrown with trees; only the large entry doors are visible. The 1940s roof height is unknown.	
Maximum View to Horizon (1940s): unknown.	

Capabilities and Purpose: Housed two 16-inch guns, largest caliber at Fort Miles and largest in the World War 2 US Army. Also housed ammunition stores and battery control elements. The photograph shows one of the casemate's roll-up entry doors.

Casemated 16-inch gun in typical Coast Artillery configuration similar to Fort Miles' Battery Smith. Note the massive concrete and mounded earth protection provided for the gun while fragile telephone lines, critical for effective fire control messages, are vulnerable to destruction by suppressive naval bombardment aimed at the casemate. (Official US Army photo in the Library of Congress)

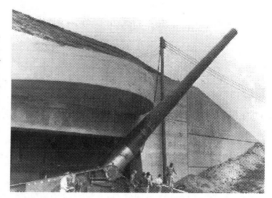

View from Tower #7 looking east over the buried 16-inch Battery Smith casemate. In the photograph, the horizon is approximately 14 miles out. The sight and sound of a two-gun salvo from Battery Smith was certainly memorable from this vantage point.

Battery Hunter Bunker	
Location: In Cape Henlopen State Park; 38-47-30N; 75- 05-32W.	
Base Height Above Sea Level: 13 feet.	
Maximum View to Horizon: 4.8 statute miles.	

Capabilities and Purpose: Controlled two 6-inch guns and housed ammunition stores, and battery control elements. The photograph shows the bunker's ocean-facing observation slit. The building survives as the base for a migratory bird observation platform and species sighted "scoreboard."

Battery Herring Bunker	
Location: At Herring Point, Cape Henlopen State Park; 38-45-95N; 75-04-97W.	
Base Height Above Sea Level: 35 feet	
Maximum View to Horizon: 8 statute miles.	

Capabilities and Purpose: Controlled two 6-inch guns and housed ammunition stores and battery control elements. The photograph shows the concrete bunker and, in the foreground, one of its two 6-inch mount positions. Battery Herring has a clear view of Towers #5 and #6 on the beach to the south.

Mobile 155mm artillery piece on the same type of Panama mount used for Fort Miles' Battery 22. Note the sand bag wall, which was the only protection available for the unshielded gun and crew.

Battery 519 Casemate	
Location: In Cape Henlopen State Park; 38-46-65N, 75-05- 22W.	
Base Height Above Sea Level: 22 feet.	
Maximum View to Horizon: 6.3 statute miles.	

Capabilities and Purpose: Originally planned to house two 16-inch guns (never delivered), the Battery 519 casemate received instead two 12-inch guns, which had been redeployed from nearby Fort Saulsbury. The casemate also enclosed an ammunition magazine and battery control elements. The photograph shows only one of two shielded gun emplacements with a 12-inch gun protruding from the southern portal of the Battery 519 casemate. This gun was acquired, restored, and installed in the casemate by the Fort Miles Historical Association in partnership with DNREC and the staff of Cape Henlopen State Park.

A 12-inch projectile store room similar to that of For Miles' Battery 519 during World War 2.

Restored Coast Artillery 8-inch gun displayed in Cape Henlopen State Park. 8-inhc guns of this type were mounted on railway flat cars. The park staff and the Fort Miles Historical Association, plan to restore an historically correct rail car for mounting this gun. Below: an 8-inch gun on one such rail car.

Restored 6-inch gun without crew-protection shield displayed in Cape Henlopen State Park. 6-inch guns were emplaced at Fort Miles at Batteries Herring and Hunter and, across the bay, at Battery 223, Cape May, New Jersey.

The wartime mine dock (now used as a fishing pier in Cape Henlopen State Park) with nearby Tower #8

Old Coast Guard Station	
Location: Cape Henlopen	
Base Height Above Sea Level: ~8 feet	
Total Tower Height Above Sea Level: estimated at ~40 feet, based on a photo of the collapsed building.	
Maximum View to Horizon: 8.5 statute miles	
Capabilities and Purpose: The building's tower was pressed into service as a Base End Station for 8-inch Railway Battery C. In 1942, the wooden building succumbed to old age and collapsed in ruin.	*Cape Henlopen Coast Guard Station after its collapse in 1942*

The Coast Artillery in Cape May, New Jersey

Tower # 23
Location: At Sunset Beach, Cape May, NJ. 38-56-63N; 74-58-02W. Tower #23 stands on the bay (western) side of Cape May Point, although its two observation slits are oriented toward the ocean.
Base Height Above Sea Level: 2 feet.
Total Tower Height Above Sea Level: 70 feet
Maximum View to Horizon: 11.4 statute miles
Capabilities and Purpose: Southern base end and spotting station for 6-inch and 155mm guns of Battery 223 at Cape May, which were very close to the Cape May Lighthouse. This tower also contributed visibility beyond the observable horizon available to the 16- and 12-inch batteries at Fort Miles. Tower 23 is open for public visitation.

Tower #24
Location: In Cape May at 38-55-97N; 74-54-47W, Beach Drive and Philadelphia Avenue. The tower was declared "war surplus" and sold with its surrounding land. Tower #24 was included in the construction of the former Golden Eagle Inn, since renamed The Grand Hotel.
Base Height Above Sea Level: 10 feet.
Total Tower Height Above Sea Level: estimated at 80 feet.
Maximum View to Horizon: 12 statute miles
Capabilities and Purpose: Northern base end and spotting station for 6-inch and 155mm guns of Battery 223 at Cape May, which were very close to the Cape May Lighthouse.

Two towers built in Wildwood and North Wildwood, New Jersey to support Battery 223 and Fort Miles' 16-inch guns, were demolished after World War 2.

Battery 223 Bunker	
Location: On the beach at Cape May at 38- 55-98N; 74-54-43W, very close to the Cape May Lighthouse.	
Base Height Above Sea Level: Battery 223 has suffered six decades of beach erosion and is presently partially submerged at high tide. The height of its former 1940s position, some 900 feet from the ocean, is unknown.	*The two cylindrical objects standing in the water to the left and right are former 6-inch gun platforms.*
Maximum View to Horizon: 1940's capability is unknown	
Capabilities and Purpose: the bunker was originally covered in sod and equipped with two 155 mm guns. Later, four 6-inch guns were added.	*View of Bunker 223 from the west, behind the beach*

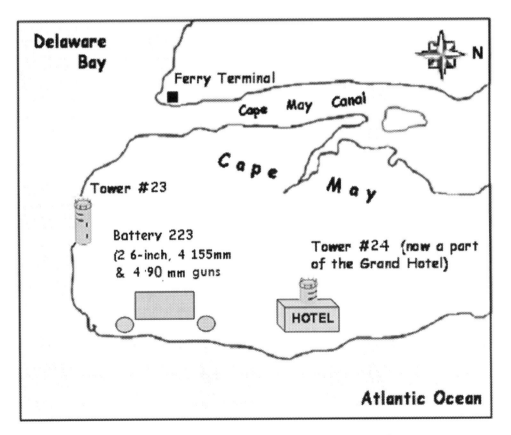

Map 3-5, surviving Fort Miles' facilities in Cape May, New Jersey.

4

The Cannoneers' Operational Challenge

View of the Target

Because of the Earth's curvature, the eyes of a male look-out of average 1940s height (5'8") standing

atop a 75-foot tall tower on a 40-foot hill or dune behind the beach (about 120 total feet above sea

level) will observe the horizon just under 13 nautical miles (14.7 statute miles in land measurement)

away.[33] This is the farthest an observer on this tower could see a ship on the horizon.[34] (See Figure 4-1).

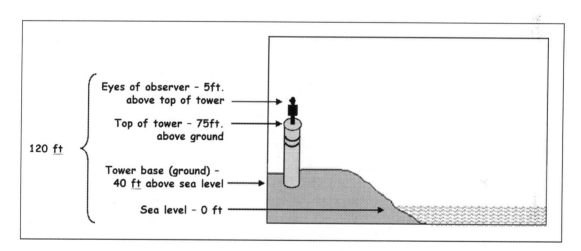

Figure 4-1, Effect of observer's height on observable horizon.

A large ship, a bit further out at sea but showing the upper 50 feet of its masts or superstructure above

the horizon, would be visible about 23 nautical miles (about 26.5 statute miles) from the tower. To a

sharp-eyed lookout scanning the horizon with telescope or binoculars, smoke rising 200 feet above

---

[33] The formula for *estimating* observed distance to the horizon: the square root of the height of the observer's eye above sea level multiplied by the constant, 1.17. The answer obtained in nautical miles can be converted to statute miles by multiplying the answer by the constant, 1.15.

[34] There are complex variables at every turn in precisely determining maximum view to the ocean horizon. Tides, which cycle twice daily between "highs" and "lows," actually describe the raising and lowering of the ocean's surface governed by moon phases and moonrise/moonset. A low ocean tide has the effect of making the top of an observation tower slightly higher (relative to the ocean surface) than at high tide and extends the view to a slightly more distant horizon. Hence footnote 28, above, refers to "estimating."

this ship would reveal its presence when the ship was just over 31 nautical miles (35.6 statute miles) out. Unfortunately, however, although Fort Miles' longest-range artillery pieces (16-inch) could fire heavy projectiles about eleven miles over the visible horizon,[35] an identifiable target could not be seen at all points within that range visually or on radar; neither could spotters mark miss-splashes occurring beyond the visible horizon. Such longer-range fire control would have depended on airborne or nearby shipborne support. These were not reliably available in 1941-42, although it had been Coast Artillery Corps doctrine since 1907 that the first information about approaching enemy ships was expected to come from off-shore scouts and pickets.[36]

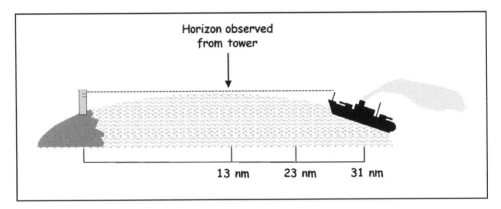

Figure 4-2, Visibility over the horizon.

At longer ranges, observers also needed to be aware of and make corrections for the effects of atmospheric refraction on their line of sight. The observing instruments were equipped with range disks that were adjusted to correspond to the instrument's height above sea level.

---

[35] The maximum range of Fort Miles' 16-inch guns was 25.5 statute miles. From the fort's tallest towers, the visible horizon was only 14.7 statute miles, a shortfall difference of 10.8 statute miles. However, the fire control towers at Cape May, New Jersey and Tower #1 just south of South Bethany, Delaware provided a partially-extended view along the coasts.

[36] C.C. Hearn, *Ibid*

"Flat" versus Highly-Arching Trajectories

19th Century technological innovations spawned two significant changes that revolutionized the use of coast artillery. The first was a near-trebling of ship speeds as sail gave way to steam. The second was the extension of artillery capabilities to ranges beyond the horizon, hence further than gunners could see.

Target Speed Complications

In the history of warfare up through the US Civil War, close-range artillery directed against advancing infantry formations employed relatively flat trajectories, where aim points were ahead of the enemy's line of march so as to send heavy iron balls bouncing into rows of men at well over 100 miles per hour. Also, through the Civil War, coastal gun crews, manning relatively small bore pieces that fired light projectiles, could handle the entire anti-ship fire mission process within *their own* resources. The speed of heavy sailing vessels was very slow, limited to no greater than what the wind and current could provide. Course changes were sluggish and abrupt evasive maneuvering not possible. Coast artillery crews could load and lay (aim) the gun, fire, observe the splash of a miss themselves, reload, correct the aim, and fire again, repeating as often as possible, so long as the target had not sailed out of range. The advantage lay with the coastal gunners and was greatly multiplied when batteries of several guns were brought to bear on the same target.

The advent of steam power, turning propeller screws, dramatically shifted the balance by seriously complicating the gunners' problems. During combat, propeller-driven ships moving *"All Ahead Full"* and zig-zagging, may be able to gain distance so quickly that the coastal gunners' aiming corrections are not helped by observing miss-splashes. This is compounded by torturously slow rates of sustained fire: an enemy ship making only 20 knots (23 statute miles per hour) could cover just over 1000 feet in the time it takes a gun crew to reload and correct its aim, if the crew's sustained rate of fire is only two rounds per minute. At longer ranges, the gun crew also may have to wait as long as 30 seconds to longer than a full minute for its last shot to impact and then calculate adjusted retargeting data, in which case the target will have moved even further.

William C. Grayson

Targets Beyond the Horizon

Improvements in 19th Century artillery technology slightly readjusted the balance between gun crews and target vessels. Longer ranges and heavier projectiles put target vessels at risk much further out to sea, theoretically over the horizon. However, guns still needed to be accurately aimed and so gun crews needed the support of artillery observers able to look further out to sea than was possible from the gun position on the ground or in a casemate. Coastal Delaware provides a good model for this situation. A Fort Miles gun crew, at battle stations with its gun on ground approximately twenty feet above sea level, sees the horizon only six miles out to sea, while the gun may have a firing range three-to-four times greater than that.

When Fort Miles' 16-inch guns were test fired to full range well over the visible horizon, Lieutenant Leonard Millar was detailed from his Coast Artillery battery at Cape May, New Jersey to a structure at nearby Wildwood Beach to observe and report the splashes of projectiles fired about one minute earlier from Fort Miles. To extend the observers' view, altitude is the answer and Fort Miles' coastal towers were put up precisely to allow observers to see a more distant horizon: the higher the observer, the more distant the horizon Observers in the towers would have used the extended view to report the positions and courses of enemy vessels as well as where the fired projectiles struck.

Especially in the 1941-1942 period of the war, aerial reconnaissance of the sea approaches to the US Atlantic coast was minimal and undependable for artillery spotting and fire control. Aircrew's naked-eye searches at night or in poor weather were nearly impossible and "look-down" airborne radar surveillance technology did not exist. Overwater aerial navigation was inexact at best and, since aircrews out of sight of land could not locate their own positions with precision, the best that could have been reported on a discovered enemy vessel was only an estimated general position totally unsuitable for artillery targeting.

The availability of effective air support would at least have provided basic target information all the way out to the maximum range of Fort Miles' big guns. For example, the fort's two 16-inch guns could fire projectiles over 25.5 statute miles; however, from the fort's tallest observation tower, ships could be seen and identified [37] no farther out than the visible horizon, which was only about 14.7 statute miles and then only from the fort's tallest towers. The southernmost of the towers (Tower #1 just below the Town of South Bethany) was erected 20 miles south from the Battery Smith casemate, which housed the 16-inch guns. Tower #1 has a horizon view of only 10.2 statute miles. It was intended to provide extended targeting support for any vessels within range of the fort's 16-inch guns and up to 10 miles out to sea from Tower #1's beach position. In the same way, the towers at Cape May and Wildwood, New Jersey provided an extended northward view beyond the horizon seen from Fort Miles. (See Chapter 3 for tower observation capabilities).

To those of us dependent on tiny calculators and personal computers operating at high speeds to solve commonplace math problems in a flash, the coast artillery targeting challenge of the early 1940s is mind-boggling. The larger-bore pieces (155mm, 6, 8, 12 and 16-inch), firing projectiles too heavy for one man to lift and load,[38] had ponderously slow rates of fire, even for the 1940s.

Well-drilled 8 and 12-inch crews could sustain no better than two rounds per minute under the best conditions while a misstep by any of the 30 to 40-member gun crew, a mechanical glitch, simple fatigue or troubling weather could reduce that rate to only one round per minute or less. In 1942, Fort Miles' 16-inch gun batteries could sustain only one round per minute in optimum circumstances.[39] Many factors slowed a gun's sustained rate of fire:

- Powder for the big guns was contained in fabric bags, such as coarse silk "shalloon," intended to burn when the gun was fired. For safety, the gun's powder chamber had to be cleared of any sparks remaining from the last shot. On older guns, powder chambers were swabbed with a wet soapy sponge[40] mounted on a long pole. Newer guns had their bores blown clear

---

[37] A battery's Fire Control would not order a fire mission against an unidentified target in US waters.

[38] The fort's 6-inch guns fired projectiles weighing 90 to 105 pounds, well within the lifting capability of a physically-conditioned soldier but, for safety and efficiency, the task was assigned to a multi-man detail.

[39] Later in the war, this was improved to three rounds per minute by updated mechanisms for moving the gun tube between shots.

[40] Army Field Manual 4-50 specified that one pound of castile soap shaved from whole bars was to be mixed with four gallons of water, then heated and gently stirred to avoid foaming.

of any sparks by compressed air tanks that discharged automatically when the gun's breech block was opened after firing.[41]

- The big projectiles were too heavy (250 to over 2200 pounds) to be lifted and put into the breech by a single soldier. A "Projectile Detail" of two to four men was needed to bring a heavy projectile to the breech on a wheeled hand truck and then to position the projectile with a mechanical device akin to an automobile jack.[42] Projectiles then had to be rammed "home" as far into the breech as they would go.

- 16- and 12-inch guns installed in the large concrete casemates were mounted on newer barbette carriages that featured electrically-powered rammers. Other guns positioned outdoors were typically rammed by a team pushing the projectile with a wooden "ram."

- To permit ramming heavy projectiles and loading bags of powder immediately behind by the "Powder Detail," gun tubes needed to be depressed (lowered) to an angle that would allow a projectile and powder bags to stay put and not begin sliding backwards before the breech was closed. Depressing and then appropriately elevating tubes for the intended range consumed much valuable time.

- Once a gun was loaded and pointed, gun section members were ordered to the rear, facing away from the gun and taking whatever protective cover was available to blunt the powerful muzzle blast. Most covered their ears during an era that predates modern "headset" ear protection and opened their mouths to equalize the pressure that would assault their eardrums.

- After the shot, the section needed some seconds to reassemble at their assigned posts. Their ears ringing and hearing at least somewhat temporarily impaired, crew members quickly resumed their battle stations in what often was a cloud of choking, eye-irritating smoke that needed friendly wind for clearance.

---

[41] The wet swabbing procedure was only required where cloth powder bags were used. On smaller artillery pieces that fired rounds consisting of powder-filled brass cases with fitted projectiles, swabbing was not needed and the rate of fire was not thereby slowed.

[42] Inside the concrete casemates, projectiles were brought to gun breeches via monorails suspended from the ceiling and were then lowered for loading by chain hoists.

- Laying (changing the azimuth) and elevating a big gun was time-consuming, adding precious seconds to the overall sequence.[43]

Ten members of a gun crew ramming a projectile into the breech. Note that the gun barrel has been lowered to save the crew from pushing the heavy projectile uphill and to keep it from sliding backward.

US Army artillery crews normally expected to hit a distant target or to hit lethally close on their third fired round, after only two corrections, but that was a *stationary or slowly moving* target on a predictable course, not a warship lurching near its top speed with evasive maneuvering possible in all 360 degrees. In practical terms, this required a tightly coordinated Coast Artillery process of dropping heavy projectiles on *predicted* enemy ship positions.

A battery's field of fire out in the ocean or inside Delaware Bay was defined by the effective range of their guns from fixed positions and as far left or right as the guns could be traversed without hitting the shoreline.[44] Although this field theoretically extends to a gun's maximum range, it is actually limited to the horizon observable by fire control spotters. This field formed an arc as shown in Figure 4-5.

Predicted target position was critical and explains why the many components of Coast Artillery are so carefully quantified. If an enemy ship had been sighted, its changing position would have been repeatedly phoned or radioed to battery plotting rooms by radar crews and visual observers in the towers. As these fixed observing locations were precisely known from carefully verified surveying, the plotting rooms would convert the incoming reports to a predicted "set forward" target position, using an early mechanical "computer" that calculated where a target ship's position was at the instant

---

[43] The 12- and 16-inch guns were equipped with electric elevating and traversing motors. 6-inch guns had only elevating motors and were traversed by hand-cranked gears.

[44] Fort Miles' 12- and 16-inch guns, emplaced in casemates, were limited to an approximate 120-degree field of fire. Outdoor 6-inch guns were mounted on ball-bearing turntables that permitted a full 360-degree field of fire.

of observation on a special plotting table. Two such examples of a plotting table were the M4 and M5 Plotting Boards.

To drop a heavy explosive projectile on any point within the battery's arc-shaped field of fire, the math had already been worked out for the plotting rooms and captured in the design of the mechanical plotting boards. The basic variables of the Coast Artillery equation were:

- the projectile weight
- range in yards to the "set forward" point at which the target was *expected* to arrive
- deflection angle (left or right) on a calculated azimuth between the gun battery and the aiming point
- the calculated weight of powder that would produce the required muzzle velocity to send the projectile the desired distance
- the elevation of the gun barrel that would extend or shorten the projectile's time of flight, considering the projectile weight and the muzzle velocity to be obtained
- the time of flight the projectile would be in the air (the longer the range, the longer the "time of flight"), ending with the precise impact time on the point at which the target was *expected* to arrive

Additional complicating variables to be considered that could significantly affect where and when a fired projectile might come down were:

- Surface winds and winds aloft, which might be blowing in different directions and at different speeds
- Barometric air pressure of the altitudes the projectile would cross (denser air at lower levels slowed a projectile much more than thinner air higher aloft)
- Temperature of the powder (affected by weather and storage conditions) that would affect the intensity and duration of the blast, which would, in turn, affect the muzzle velocity obtained. Temperature was expected to vary significantly by the hour but the most trustworthy means of verifying powder came to be accepted as carefully observing actual results obtained from firing the artillery piece.

- Number of times the piece had been fired since it was last "ranged" in a test, as each shot very slightly wore down the barrel's interior rifling, affecting the tube's maximum compression and resulting muzzle velocity.

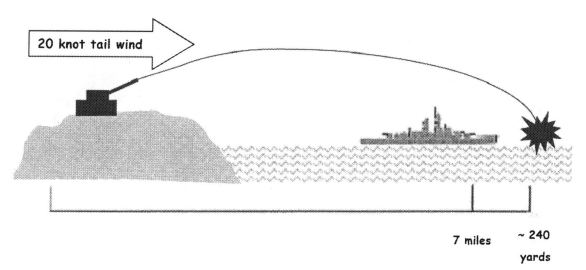

Figure 4-3, A 20-knot "tail wind" could cause a heavy projectile to overshoot its intended target by as much as 240 yards.

The effects of winds on in-flight projectiles was a well-understood problem. Coast Artillery regiments had full-time Meteorological Sections that measured wind directions and speeds with helium-filled weather balloons released near the beach, updating the plotting rooms as conditions changed.

With these known variables established as accurately as possible, battery commanders needed to monitor where the gun crews were in their loading sequences and, based on experience, predict when – in elapsed seconds – each gun would be ready to fire. Usually, both guns of a battery would be fired simultaneously relying on probability that one of the projectiles would hit the target. With that piece of the puzzle in place, cannoneers would be given the range in yards and the deflection in degrees of arc and would report when the loaded gun was properly layed.[45]

The battery commander's order to fire, considering the projectile's known flight time and the predicted arrival of the enemy ship at the "set forward" point, would be timed for target and projectiles to converge.

---

[45] The standard military convention of the day was to express range in "yards" because "feet" was too granular a measurement to be useful and "miles" was too coarse. In this analysis, ranges are discussed in miles and fractions of miles as a convenience to those readers unaccustomed to thinking in terms of thousands of yards.

Unlike the infantry, which can visually observe the impacts of rifle and machine gun bullets split-seconds after firing, this instant feedback is not available to artillery crews.

Quite the opposite; artillery projectiles are fired along very high arcs and battery controllers usually have enough time to advise forward observers by radio or telephone that a fire mission has been executed by speaking the voice message, *"Shot on Way."* Although more pertinent to Field Artillery operations, the 261st Coast Artillery Regiment adopted this traditional gunners' message as a motto for its National Guard unit badge.

The "time of flight" of an artillery projectile fired at a distant target is very likely the most challenging variable in the plotting calculation. In Table 4-1, below, the shortest possible projectile flight time considers only a straight line-of-sight from the gun to the target, which is, of course, impossible to achieve under the laws of physics.

Long range artillery fire missions measured in miles can be attained only via very high, arching trajectories in which the climb to and descent from the highest point (the apogee) adds substantial time. The token times given in Table 4-1 are included here only for simplified illustration. There are too many complicating variables to consider for a simplified example here.

Table 4-1, Projectile Time of Flight

Gun	Muzzle Velocity (feet per second)	View to Observed Horizon	Shortest Possible Time of Flight to Visible Horizon
16-inch	2750	14.7 statute miles *	28.2 seconds
12-inch	2250	14.7 statute miles *	34.5 seconds
8-inch	2600[†]	14.7 statute miles *	29.8 seconds
6-inch	2598	14.7 statute miles *	29.8 seconds
155mm	2710	14.7 statute miles*	28.8 seconds

* Nominal view from tallest Base End Towers at Fort Miles
† Average of several available projectile weights

The extremely challenging targeting process for big guns firing at long ranges explains why it was a standard combat tactic for capital ships to fire multi-gun salvoes at moving enemy ships during a naval battle. Against a moving target, the probability is low of a hit by a single shot that could be in the air nearly a half-minute or even quite longer. The "hit" probability, however, is greatly increased by a six or nine-gun "broadside," employing "shotgun" principles that hope for at least one of the projectiles to find its mark.

The most relevant example in the early days of World War 2 was remembered from the World War 1 Battle of Jutland in 1916. While under way, the Royal Navy's Grand Fleet fired 1539 rounds from their big guns, with only 5% hitting their targets. Only 3% of the maneuvering German High Seas Fleet's 1904 shots found their marks.

The temptation to consider "what if" scenarios is compelling. Against a multi-ship flotilla maneuvering in formation offshore but close enough to be seen or against enemy landing craft approaching the beach, coastal cannoneers most likely would have given a good account of themselves. However, individual combatant enemy vessels rigged for battle and attacking in small numbers would have been expected to strike in the dark, move at flank speed, make smoke, and zig-zag to hamper targeting by coastal guns as much as possible. Visibility reduced by rain or fog would also have added to already complicated targeting problems.

From the moment fast enemy ships were positively identified as having entered Fort Miles' visible zone of responsibility – just under 15 miles from shore in the best case – they could have reached the mouth of Delaware Bay in approximately 30 minutes. Those 30 minutes would have framed a frantic scramble that tested the full range of regimental warfighting capabilities and readiness plus the courage and discipline of gun crews exposed in the open to counter-battery fire.

Making something near 25 knots on evasive courses, enemy ships would be covering almost a half-mile per minute or about 42 feet per second. If a target's actual arrival at the point a gun was aimed to hit was only five seconds earlier or later than the battery's plotted calculation, the projectile would hit the water some 210 feet away from the target. As seen from Table 4-1, above, the shortest (but actually impossible) elapsed time between long-distance firing (to the observed horizon) and an observed "hit" or "splash" was approximately 30 seconds but in reality was much longer. At closer ranges (e.g., ten miles), the muzzles of the bigger guns would have been depressed and projectile times of flight would have been significantly shorter.

Enemy vessels approaching to within ten miles of the mouth of Delaware Bay would also have been engaged by the fort's 3-inch and 90mm guns with higher sustained rates of fire. These smaller guns, intended primarily to engage fast motor torpedo boats, would not be expected, though, to knock a heavily-armored combatant vessel out of action. However, against close-in targets,[46] fire controllers in Tower #9 (near the tip of Cape Henlopen) would have been able to observe the impacts of 3-inch/90mm projectiles very soon after they were fired and make aiming corrections quickly. Nevertheless, any direct hits by the bigger guns would have been very great achievements but even "near misses," which drove a powerful salt water shock wave against a ship's hull, were capable of damaging vital but fragile rudders and propellers.

Had visibility allowed the sighting of multiple enemy vessels within a 10-mile field of fire, the 21st Coast Artillery was capable of awesome firepower once it had attained its 1943 high point. The 40 guns at Fort Miles and Cape May had a potential of putting 117 explosive projectiles per minute (or just under two per second) into that smaller battle area. This sobering strength would have posed a difficult challenge for German naval attack planners and would have made for a very tense ride for *Kriegsmarine* skippers instinctively ordering zig-zagging course changes.

No US Army Coast Artillery gun battery based in the Continental US fired a shot in anger during World War 2.[47] Without an historical record to consult, we can only guess at the probable outcome of an attempted dash into Delaware Bay on a cold, rainy night by multiple armed surface combatants of the *Kriegsmarine*, supported by suppressive fire aimed at Fort Miles' emplacements. Assuming the minefields stretching across the mouth of the bay's shipping channel had not in some way been neutralized, they represented a highly formidable defensive layer backing up the cannoneers. Once

---

[46] Under ten statute miles

[47] US Marine Coast Artillerymen defending Wake Island with 5-inch guns during the December 1941 Japanese invasion sunk the destroyer *Hayate*. The Marines also set a troopship afire, damaged the destroyer *Yayoi* and the invasion flagship cruiser *Yuban*. The Japanese withdrew when their flagship was damaged. *Hayate* was the first ship of the Japanese Navy to be sunk in World War 2 and the Marines' coastal gunnery was principally responsible for the only defeat of an amphibious landing by either side during the entire war. The Japanese returned, however, and eventually took Wake Island with a larger invasion force.

past the Fort Miles and Cape May defenses, however, enemy vessels would have been engaged at closer range in a much narrower part of the bay: first by the guns of Fort Saulsbury and then by Forts Dupont and Delaware (on Peapatch Island) plus any additional resources the Navy, Coast Guard, and Army Air Force were able to throw into the battle. This defense-in-depth potential would have been a discouraging deterrent to German naval planners.

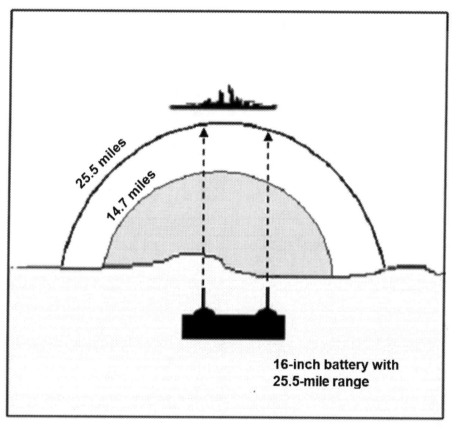

Figure 4-5, A battery's area of responsibility was determined by the effective range of its guns but effectively limited by the observable distance available to the fire control system.

Coast Artillerymen drilled continuously, striving to shave seconds from the process of identifying an off-shore target, pinpointing its location and predicting its movements, loading and pointing the big guns, firing at their targets, adjusting azimuth and range and reloading. It was not expected that enemy ships would hold slow, steady courses, making it easy for the gunners. Tactical air support, perhaps by seaplanes carried on enemy ships, was also considered a possibility that included bombing and strafing the fort's artillery emplacements, storage facilities and gun crews caught in the open.

The gunners' challenge was complex. Visibility at night or in rain or fog would have degraded the ability to recognize friend from foe. Radar in the early 1940s, typified by Fort Miles' SCR- 296 sets, was in its technological infancy. However, the SCR-296s would have permitted gun laying in the dark and in reduced daylight visibility but could not contribute to target identification and the separation of enemy targets from any friendly vessels.

Meteorological Section about to launch a weather balloon and track it with an optical instrument.

Finding and Fixing the Targets

Visual Observation and Triangulation

To effectively point Fort Miles' Coast Artillery guns, targets had to be very accurately measured in terms of azimuth (where to point) and range (how far out). Spotters in the observation towers fought the war with very high resolution optical instruments.

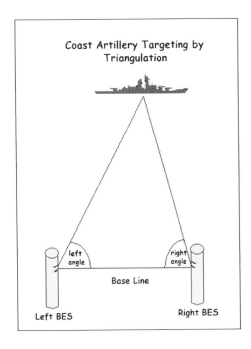

Through their observation slits going one-third of the way around, Fort Miles' towers afforded unobstructed ocean views out to a more distant horizon than was possible from sea level or atop the beach dunes. Observations from any of the towers were telephoned to battery plotting rooms via a manually-operated switchboard and any two towers up and down the beach could serve as Base End Stations (BESs). A precisely surveyed line between any two towers of a pair was the "Base Line" and each of the towers was a "Base End." Lines were also precisely measured from the BESs to the main gun or "directing point" of each supported battery. (See the illustrations later in this chapter).

Up in the towers at the observation levels, soldiers with binoculars and azimuth instruments were trained to spot and recognize potential targets all the way out to the horizon and slightly beyond, if a ship's masts or smoke could be seen above the horizon. The most critical duty of these troops was to very accurately acquire an enemy target with the optical device and report its azimuth as a line of bearing from his tower.

The standard Army Model 1910A-1 azimuth telescope was installed in pairs in each tower; one for spotting and one for tracking. Soldiers on the spotting instrument were tasked with observing miss-splashes and reporting distance from the aiming point. The instruments were on mounts that supported the telescope and contained elevating, leveling and azimuth measuring mechanisms.

The towers were not equipped with interior lighting so that they could not be themselves targeted by enemy ships at night. After sunset, the troops had to work for long periods in the dark, relying on very small battery-operated illumination on instruments' graduated scales.

Tracker and Reader using a Model 1910A-1 Azimuth
Instrument. Note the ship recognition charts.

Two soldiers were assigned to each "tracking" instrument; an "operator" and a "reader." With a target ship in the tracking telescopes' field of view, the "reader" could read two scales: one showing the azimuth to the target being tracked in degrees and the other scale showing hundredths of degrees. Readings were taken each time a centrally-controlled time-interval bell sounded the third of three "dings" throughout the battery.[48] Reporting metered by the bells assured that azimuths were read simultaneously in both Base End Towers. This procedure avoided situations in which two observers might report azimuths to the same moving ship at slightly different times and positions. If that happened, the target would actually have been reported at two different positions, throwing-off the calculated aiming point.

The tempo of the "Position Finding Cycle" was standardized to provide efficiency without tiring the observers, who might be involved in long periods of tracking. The training manuals establish a goal of 20 to 40 seconds for observers as satisfactory.

Target Identification and Reporting

The selection of targets and command to open fire depended critically on the availability of the best information available and the analytic skills of battery's team members, including observers, readers, spotters, and men around the plotting tables. Besides determining positively that a potential target was an enemy vessel, the battery needed to assure that the gun crew would aim at the same ship that had been reported by two different observers.

It was critically important to know with certainty that both observers were focused on the same target ship and not two different ones. To simplify the description of potential targets, ships were classified by the number of funnels and masts (referred to as "stacks and sticks.") visible in their silhouettes. A ship with one funnel and one mast was a "Class 1-1" vessel; a "Class 3-2" had three funnels and two masts, likelier a large ship.

---

[48] It was standard Coast Artillery procedure that guns would also have been fired on the third "ding."

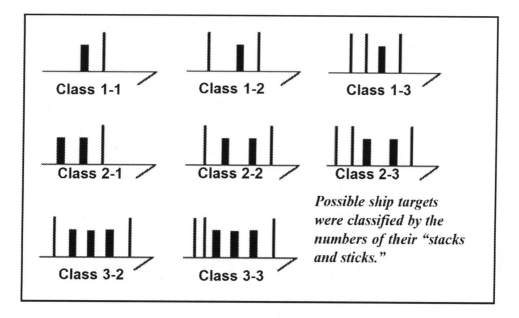

Class 1-1   Class 1-2   Class 1-3

Class 2-1   Class 2-2   Class 2-3

Class 3-2   Class 3-3

Possible ship targets were classified by the numbers of their "stacks and sticks."

A part of the azimuth reporting process was coordination between observer crews in adjacent towers on which ship they were watching. Reports were telephoned from each Base End Station (BES) to the battery's plotting room, updating the observed azimuth.

The towers supporting shorter range 6-inch or smaller guns were also equipped with optical stereoscopic range finders such as the Army's standard M9, similar to the rangefinders of some single lens reflex cameras. Initially, two images of a vessel would be seen but, as the rangefinder was adjusted, the two moved together, overlapping to become a single sharp image. The range to the target could then be read and telephoned to the plotting room.

Some observation towers were also equipped with depression range finding instruments. With the height from the tower base very precisely known, a special telescope focused on a target ship would measure the angle at which it was depressed from level. Using these two values, the distance from the tower to the target could be geometrically determined and reported to the plotting room; however, results were less accurate than the triangulation process based on azimuths measured at BESs.

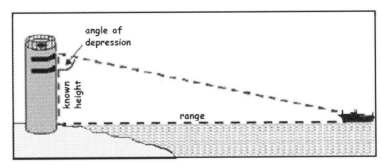

Figure 4-4, Calculating range by measuring Angle of Depression

 *"Plotting Board," a large round, disk on table legs. Plotters received telephoned azimuth reports and positioned moveable "arm" pointers. The Plotting Board, was equipped with moveable drafting machines and attached straight-edge rulers. Around the table's edge was a graduated azimuth scale from zero to 360°. As reports were received by telephone or radio, the drafting machines' rulers were used to draw lines from positions representing the reporting BESs and their observed azimuths. In this photo, reenactors from the Fort Miles historical Association demonstrate the targeting process.*

A "gun arm" was used to draw a line from the battery's "main gun" to the plotted target position and had a "range scale" engraved on its length. A "set forward" distance was calculated to allow for the target's speed and a fired projectile's time of flight to derive the gun's pointing azimuth.

Soldiers in the towers were assigned to specific battery "Range Sections." In towers with two observation levels, the upper level was used to support batteries with longer-range guns. (The tables in Chapter 3 describe the operational association of towers with specific gun batteries or minefields, as appropriate).

Intra-Battery Communications

Although the landline telephone, such as the EE-8 pictured below, was designated as the primary equipment, radios, flags, signal lamps, and messengers were also available. The *Signal Communications* training manuals describe a highly structured and standardized signaling process that linked the various players in the battery. Local net discipline was enforced to enhance efficiency and the manuals list numerous rules such as:

- how to pronounce letters and numbers phonetically
- encouragement to raise the voice slightly when necessary but never to shout
- avoidance of unnecessary conversation, and
- speaking civilly to the switchboard operator.

Type EE-8 field telephone was in common use among Fort Miles' towers and battery plotting rooms.

Battery operator at tactical telephone switch

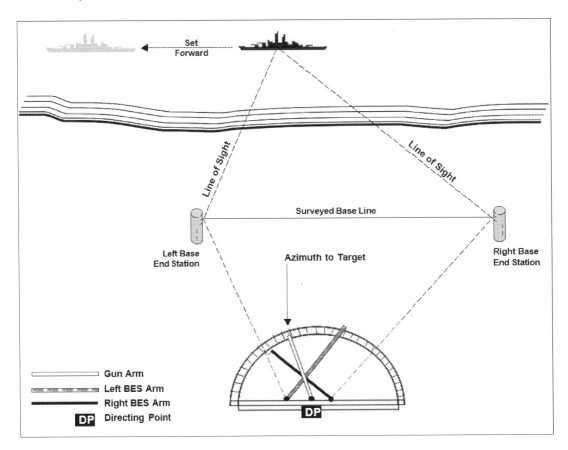

Figure 4-5, Use of the Plotting Board for targeting by triangulation. The azimuths reported by observers in both the Left and Right Base End Stations (BESs) at the third "ding" of the central timing bell are used to set the Left and Right BES Arms on the plotting board's graduated edge. The Gun Arm is positioned at the point where the two BES arms cross and the azimuth the Gun Arm indicates on the board's edge is the targeting azimuth from the battery's Directing Point. Additional reports of the target ship's course and speed will be used with the expected "flight time" of fired projectiles to calculate a "Set Forward" Point, which is the predicted point at which the target ship and projectiles would simultaneously arrive.

5

Soldiering at Wartime Fort Miles

By mid-1942, Fort Miles was quickly growing into a major US Army installation, with a mix of both commonplace and unique facilities. Heavy construction would continue well into 1943. In the "unique" facility category were the massive reinforced concrete artillery casemates (the largest buildings on the post), the Fire Control Towers (the tallest), and a Mine Dock 1800-foot-long, with a sometimes-present visiting US Army minelaying vessel moored to it. Among the customary Army post facilities were a mix of standard wooden and concrete administrative buildings, motor pools and workshops, barracks, mess halls, Post Exchange (PX), chapel, theater, and a 118-bed clinic, all bustling with a population of 2500. Half-buried ammunition storage "igloos," various bunkers, and "cable huts" dotted the fort. Back from the oceanfront dunes, Fort Miles' appearance was typical of stateside Army installations undergoing a major upgrade. Troops in regulation olive drab fatigues [49] and Coast Artillery blue dungarees plus assorted military vehicles and construction equipment completed the moving picture.

At its peak strength, Fort Miles' Coast Artillery units consisted of:

Unit	Officers	Warrant Officers	Enlisted
21st CAR	28	3	551
261st CAB	30	3	576
Mine Planting Battery	1	6	42

The post was home to a Regular Army regiment and its subordinate brigades, managed by long-service senior officer commanders and staffs, who took their responsibilities very seriously. Fort Miles was at war on the front line of homeland defense and all military personnel assigned to Fort Miles up to the end of August 1945 were awarded the American Campaign Medal. Accordingly, the senior officers set the tone of standard

---

[49] The old word "fatigues" has been replaced by "Battle Dress Uniform" (BDUs).

Army wartime discipline over every aspect of a soldier's life. Exercising command down through a chain that extended to young officers and more mature sergeants, garrison duty was highly structured and tightly scheduled, relying on live bugle calls to signal the start of activities as well as the day's closing moments.

Identification with a "team" and the fostering of teamwork are fundamental goals of all military organizations. Maintaining soldiers' physical health and combat readiness is another basic goal set in motion by centuries of hard lessons learned about how quickly and broadly debilitating sickness can start and spread among troops living in very close conditions.

Developing teamwork and staying healthy were behind most of the routine daily activities that kept a soldier busy. In addition to practicing on and maintaining their assigned artillery and support systems, soldiers marched in squad and company formations, cleaned their barracks and latrines to near-perfection, kept their rifles and themselves clean and close-shaven and stood open-ranks inspection as units. Unsatisfactory performance by one soldier or a few typically resulted in discipline of the whole team. Soldiers were trained to pull together and the group was trained in self-help to encourage its lower performers toward excellence.

21st Coast Artillery troops preparing for open-ranks inspection.
In response to the order, "Dress Right," each man has extended
his left arm marking the required space between them.

The pre-war life-experience of the typical soldier, who had enlisted or was drafted, included living with his parents during the dispiriting and prolonged Great Depression[50], attending high school, and perhaps, brief employment in an entry-level job, if he had been lucky enough to find one. The Delaware National Guard troops averaged a couple of years older, coming mostly from nearby farms and towns. They had a bit more part-time military experience and artillery familiarity than most draftees and enlistees. The National Guard troops tended to know friends and neighbors with whom they had served pre-war weekend drills as opposed to the regulars who found their way to Fort Miles individually from many states.

Off-duty time wasn't necessarily free time. Soldiers needed a pass measured in hours to leave the post [51] and were frequently assigned to work onerous details such as KP,[52] picking up cigarette butts and other trash, or janitorial tasks. They went to bed, arose, and ate meals together on set schedules timed by standard Army bugle calls. In addition to the time-honored practice of keeping soldiers busy as a way of keeping them out of trouble, the regiment was at Readiness Condition II from Pearl Harbor Day through most of 1942. At Readiness Condition II, whole gun crews needed to stay at or near their combat duty posts. In the event of a combat situation, full-strength gun sections would have double-timed to their battle stations. Not knowing the whereabouts of one or more absent section members would have been intolerable for squad and section leaders. Any delay of a gun section's achievement of readiness to fire that was caused by a soldier not promptly answering the call to battle stations would have been severely disciplined.

Although they are upscale seaside resorts today, nearby Lewes, Dewey, Rehoboth and Bethany Beach represented small-town America in the early 1940s, concentrating on maritime and agricultural industries.

Separated from the Baltimore-Washington area by Chesapeake Bay, the area would not develop into a popular beach resort until the construction of a bridge across the bay in 1952. Most Delaware locals

---

[50] 1929-1941

[51] Troops returning late from a pass had the period of lateness deducted from their next pass.

[52] KP = "Kitchen Police" and included potato peeling, washing and drying mess hall cooking and table utensils. Some daily details away from operational assignments were avoided by the hiring of local civilian labor for mess halls.

actively supported the war effort and patriotic civic programs such as bond drives, minimizing consumption of scarce commodities, and turning in reusable materials at collection centers. They accepted rationing, dim-outs, and the rumbles and vibrations of Fort Miles' big gun test firings.

Soldiers on pass were welcome in the local towns as they sought beer, contact with girls, and temporary respite from the discipline of Army life. Local civilians generally had a positive view of "their" Army post and adopted a parental attitude to the troops. Delaware newspapers of the time do not contain editorials or letters-to-editors worrying that Fort Miles might subject nearby civilian areas to danger during an enemy attack.

World War 2 ration stamps

An unfortunate setback to community relations was caused by a misunderstood Fort Miles announcement of a July 4, 1942 "Open House." Numerous disappointed local townsfolk, hopeful of a peek behind the scenes, were turned back at the main gate, if they were not family members of a GI stationed on post.

Masthead of the Ft. Miles post newspaper, Coastal Bursts, featuring a casemated artillery piece.

The regiment, calling itself simply the "21st Coast Artillery," published mimeographed[53] and strictly censored weekly newspapers, *Time Table* and *Coastal Bursts* limited very carefully to non-operational subjects. No articles revealed the numbers and types of artillery weapons on-post and no information was ever reported on any aspect of the regiment's combat capabilities. On its masthead, *Time Table* featured the regimental slogan, "*In Adjustment*," calling attention to the transformation of life from "democratic status" to Army discipline and the constant adjustment of the fort's weapons and support systems.

---

[53] Mimeographing: an obsolete document reproducing technology in which a thin wax "stencil" sheet was typed by a typewriter whose keys were set to strike the stencil directly and not through a typewriter ribbon. The keys perforated the wax in the shape of letters and numbers and the stencil was then wrapped around an inked drum which forced ink through the perforations onto blank paper. Mimeographs were replaced by photocopiers in the late 1950s.

Most of the paper's weekly coverage was focused on commanding officers' and chaplains' inspirational messages, information about how to send money home to family members, bantering gossip that teased what come across as popular NCOs and news of on-post entertainment and intramural sports.

Much of what is taken for granted in our modern age was absent and undreamt of in the early 1940s. No soldier had ever seen a television and radios, which were few and far between, tended to be furniture-sized AM receivers. There were no small portables for entertainment. Very few post buildings had telephones and no soldier had a personal telephone he could carry in a pocket.

Long-distance telephone calling was all operator-assisted, relatively expensive, and usually reserved by families for emergency notification. Western Union telegrams could be sent from local towns but they, too, were usually sent only with bad news. Families with loved-ones in service would be made instantly fearful, if a Western Union messenger carrying a yellow envelope approached, and soldiers subconsciously understood that telegrams were to be avoided. Mail was the principal means of communication for soldiers; incoming letters were usually handed-out in "mail call" formations. Soldiers were permitted to send letters free of postage but were always aware that their outgoing letters were subject to security review and censorship.

Official Army teletype messages could travel no faster than sixty words per minute. News arrived via AM radio, if you were near one, by local newspaper,[54] if you could buy or borrow one, or by the word-of-mouth "grapevine." Newspapers, even though days old, were highly valued as information sources. The computer had only just been invented in England to analyze intercepted German cipher messages, was a closely-guarded secret, and no soldier at Fort Miles even knew what a computer was.

The first ballpoint pens were not sold in the US until after the war in October 1945 and sold for $12.50 at a time when skilled labor earned only 25¢ per hour. Writing or signing papers in ink were usually performed at desks or tables with pen points dipped in bottled ink. "Fountain pens," filled from bottles of ink, were carried by a few in shirt pockets, were expensive, and frequently leaked large, ruinous stains. Pencils were a soldier's most-carried writing instruments.

---

[54] Newspapers from Wilmington and Philadelphia came down to Lewes by train and were sold locally. The towns of Lewes and Rehoboth also had hometown newspapers that carried national and war news.

William C. Grayson

In administrative offices and battery orderly rooms, soldiers who knew how to type, prepared all of the regiment's official documents. Typing ability was a valuable skill that kept the clerks out of battery gun crews. The Army did not use electric typewriters and, as most official documents were needed in multiple copies, clerks separated pages with carbon paper. Typing mistakes had to be patiently erased from the original and each carbon copy.

As a pastime, casual trooper conversations and traditional group "gripe sessions" were pervasive. War rumors about the threat of imminent combat, possible unit or individual soldier deployment overseas, and how men wanted to believe they would perform in action were common subjects alongside talk of things missed at home, baseball, complaints about chow and the unfairness of sergeants. News of off-shore U-Boat attacks, German saboteur landings on Long Island and Florida beaches, and Japanese submarine shellings of West coast facilities fueled excited discussion and kept most of the troops on edge.

Aside from radio programs or a movie in the post theater, leisure and entertainment were simple and locally-organized. The troops gambled at cards or dice and played baseball, basketball, and touch football. Soccer was basically unknown in the US and the post gym had a boxing ring and basketball court but none of the fitness equipment we know today. Ping pong tournaments were organized but there was no bowling alley, golf course, tennis courts or swimming pool. Summertime dips in the ocean surf at designated points on the beach were greatly enjoyed.[55]

---

[55] Towers # 5 and 6 are immediately north of a stretch of sand called "Whiskey Beach." Although the exact derivation of the name has been lost in time, a historical marker suggests the possibility that soldiers from Fort Miles used this part of the beach for recreational purposes.

Harbor Defenses of the Delaware March

We're the harbor defenses of the Delaware.
We keep watch over land and the sea.
If we are to have peace, we are well aware
That this country must have victory.

Two talented NCOs wrote
a regimental march,
whose lyrics survive.

We will fight with the might that will keep us free
From the tyrants who covet our shores.
We will crush their armies,
Sink their navies,
Shoot them from the air
In defense of our Delaware.

- Lyrics by Sergeants Mark
Laub and Jesse Berkman

Fitness was maintained through NCO-led calisthenics outdoors and double-time marching with full backpack and rifle. All members of the regiment were drilled in standard infantry tactics and practiced marksmanship on a rifle range between beachfront sand dunes. No one jogged individually and bicycles were a form of essential point-to-point transportation for those who had them, usually not recreational fitness equipment.

Horses also provided some local transportation and Ed Riggin, Sr., whose Dewey Beach [56] restaurant parking lot used to sport a concrete model fire control tower, has childhood memories of mounted soldiers riding among various military facilities near the beach.

Photography wasn't the serious hobby it is today; fixed-focus/fixed exposure personal cameras were very simple. Shooting size 126 black and white film, small cameras of the period were satisfactory for souvenir sunlit snapshots and, in common with US GIs everywhere, the soldiers of Fort Miles recorded piles of photos of proud kids in uniform, often in small groups of close buddies. For security,

---

[56] Ed's Chicken & Crabs on Delaware Route 1 at Swedes St.

cameras were banned from operational areas and the archives contain only official photographs of weaponry and support assets.

Sgt. Charles West, 21st CAR, and barrack-mates pose inside their sparely furnished quarters. Note the coal stove and the absence of windows, closets and any place to seek privacy.

Music was available if there were a radio nearby and a few talented troops could entertain their buddies with harmonicas or guitars. A phonograph playing 78rpm records was an uncommon luxury. No soldier knew what cassette tapes, CDs or iPods were. Group singing was common in the Army of World War 2 and a popular song that brought the barracks to full voice was a reassuring sign to officers and NCOs of high morale. Visiting USO musical shows, often outdoors and using a flat bed truck as a stage, were especially appreciated by all ranks.

Pizza delivery and fast-food carry-outs would not come on the scene for another 20 years. Because of wartime shortages and the interruption of non-essential commodity imports, coffee, candy bars and chewing gum disappeared from shops and many kitchen staples were rationed. Troops in barracks and at their duty stations shared these inconveniences with the general population.[57] Fort Miles' gun

---

[57] Fort Miles troops were exhorted to be careful in their consumption of food and were constantly reminded of the shortages being experienced in the civilian population.

installations, tall towers, and plotting rooms were not equipped with office coffee makers or water coolers. Observers in the fire control towers made do without electricity, running water, and indoor toilets.[58] Soldiers carried with them what they would need during a duty shift in water canteens and thermos bottles. Meals eaten at duty stations were frequently unpopular pre-packaged "K-Rations" or were delivered by truck from mess halls, if the men were lucky.

Chaplain (Captain) Bishop (standing) in a combination chapel and recreation room at Fort Miles. The troops had access to newspapers, books and simple board games.

In the early 1940s, there were no personal deodorants, no sunblock, and no insect repellant sprays. In the summertime, temperatures and humidity soared indoors. Air conditioning was found only in big city motion picture theaters and all the movies would have been rated "G." Sticky flypaper hung in many buildings and in all mess hall kitchens, which were only partly successful at keeping insects from joining official Army recipes.

Soldiers assigned to outdoor details or sentry patrols were plagued by biting sand flies and were tormented by various other stinging insects that arrived on westerly winds. Painful, peeling sunburns were expected summertime experiences.

---

[58] Tower #8, located adjacent to the main road into Lewes, was an exception with electricity installed.

Batteries were billeted together in barracks clustered with mess halls and administrative buildings close-by their assigned battle stations in casemates or the open-air emplacements. If directed to go to battle stations by bugle call, whistles, or shouted commands, they would have grabbed their helmets and double-timed the short distances.

Barracks had no refrigerators and microwave ovens wouldn't arrive for thirty years. Ice cubes were a rare luxury. Soft drinks were chilled by ice water in large metal boxes bearing the logos of major national brands and depended on deliveries of blocks of ice. A very few of these would be found in the nearby towns; coin-operated machines dispensing cold bottled or canned drinks were unknown. Tap water was universally drunk; faucet-mounted filters were unknown and there was no bottled "spring" water.

Sleep in leaky tents and later in wooden barracks on humid summer nights was often difficult. World War 2 "open bay" barracks housed rows of bunks on both sides of a long room. Privacy was viewed by the Army as an enemy of unit cohesion so barrack-mates slept, showered, and used toilets in plain view of each other. The idea of co-ed billeting would have been viewed as preposterous. Soldiers stood elbow-to-elbow at rows of sinks to brush their teeth and shave in lather worked-up using shaving brushes. Most troops used a straight razor that lasted for years, if frequently stropped on a leather belt.

Warrant Officer Ralph H. Trader, Jr. remembers the post maintaining a total nighttime blackout to deny enemy ships any aiming points and to keep from silhouetting friendly vessels passing off-shore. He recalls the possibility of sudden *Kriegsmarine* shelling being taken very seriously. Up in the cylindrical concrete towers on 8-hour watches, the troops roasted in the summer sunshine and, in a time when nearly every young man smoked, had to exercise care every night of the year not to permit a match or glowing cigarette to be seen from inside a tower's observation slits. Although many of the towers were within sight of each other, troops needed to resist the temptation to signal to neighboring observers by flashlight, lest they violate the blackout.

Typical shower room (left) and communal latrine (right). Note the side-by-side wooden-covered commode seats. [Post-war photos taken long after daily cleaning by GIs].

Climbing as many as 150 rungs of a ladder[59] while loaded with personal equipment in an overheated tower had most men dripping sweat by the time they reached their assigned duty levels. During warm weather evenings, being able to get on the tower roof to take in the ocean breeze under the stars was a special treat. In the winter, however, bone-chilling coastal fog and cold wind blowing stinging sand kept the troops inside the towers, which were, at least, comfortably heated.

Staying alert in a cylindrical tower only 17 feet in diameter with narrow observation slits for windows was difficult day-after-day on 8-hour shifts broken only for meal and latrine necessities. Every vessel spotted on the horizon (and each turned out to be friendly) was routinely tracked as a potential artillery target both to practice battery coordination and to relieve boredom. Good visibility out to sea and left to right along the beach was reassuring to a sense of personal safety while darkness, mist and rain brought feelings of edginess and frustration.

Soldiers in Tower #1 at the southernmost end of the regiment's installations were glad to be able to see Tower #2 in their binoculars, five miles to the north and enthusiastically welcomed the arrival of any vehicle bringing food or their relief as a change in the routine. The troops in Tower #2 were also well south of the main fort but were able to at least keep an eye on Tower #3, six miles to the north, as their nearest connection to the main base. Even today, with the nearby presence of residential dwelling and street lights, the Tower #1 and #2 locations are surrounded in spooky blackness on dark nights.

---

[59] The equivalent of climbing 10 to 12 flights of stairs

Although Fort Miles' main mission is remembered as anti-ship, the regiment was also tasked to defend against any enemy aircraft crossing the coast from seaward and mounted numerous Anti-Aircraft batteries all over the post. The interior walls of the towers were decorated with recognition posters for both enemy and friendly ships and aircraft.

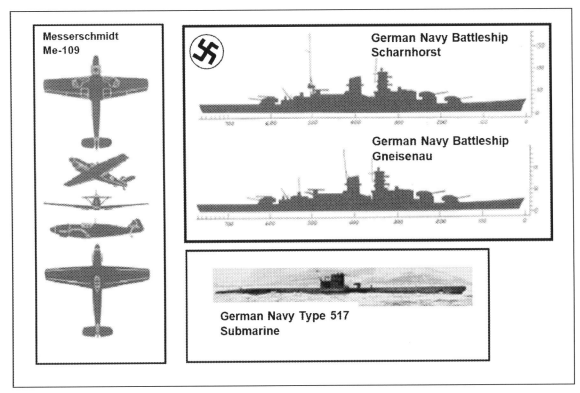

German recognition silhouettes

6

Fort Miles Stands Down

As Admiral Yamamoto correctly predicted immediately after the Pearl Harbor attack, the US giant awoke from a neglectful slumber and very swiftly began implementing a powerful resolve, shifting into high gear by the summer of 1942. The three Axis powers, which had overrun and enslaved weaker neighbors, immediately began to succumb to Allied counteroffensives fueled by the military and industrial might of the US. By the autumn of 1942, less than a year after Pearl Harbor and only two months after a series of disheartening US tactical defeats everywhere, the Axis invaders were stopped cold or were in retreat on all fronts. US confidence was high and Winston Churchill cautiously surmised that the Allies had reached "the end of the beginning" of the war.[60] To be sure, the enemy was still capable of delivering fanatical, lethal blows highlighted by the German's Battle of the Bulge offensive and V1 and V2 rocket attacks plus Japan's stubborn resistance on hard-won Pacific islands and costly *Kamikaze* attacks. Still, news reports of steady Allied progress translated to a reduction in the likelihood of an attack on US coasts and an easing of tensions felt by Coast Artillery troops.

Although German U-Boats would continue to prey upon Allied vessels in the Atlantic, vastly improved US naval and air capabilities made the Atlantic coastal area too risky for any *Kriegsmarine* surface vessels and their hunting grounds were pushed well to the east. In those changed circumstances, the War Department reassessed the threat to the homeland and concluded on October 29, 1942:

- Remotely probable: attack by a major Axis fleet
- Improbable: commando-type actions
- Probable: isolated raids by submarine and light vessels.

These conclusions were only estimates so, as a back-up, the Coast Artillery was kept at a high state of readiness through the winter of 1942-43. By spring, however, the War Department was more confident and declared a "State of Non-Invasion" for the New York-Philadelphia Sector in April 1943.

---

[60] November 10, 1942

In a few weeks, Eastern Defense Command lowered the sector's readiness posture to "Defense B."[61] Attention by then had become more sharply focused on foreign fronts, which would need the support of qualified cannoneers. Plans made earlier for redeploying troops overseas from Fort Miles and other Coast Artillery installations were approved and the 21st Coast Artillery Regiment and 261st Coast Artillery Brigade at Fort Miles were designated "Limited Service Units." Many soldiers of the Regular Army and the Delaware National Guard shipped-out of Fort Miles to join Army Field Artillery batteries in Europe and the Far East.

World War 2 Victory Medal

The fort's newspaper, *Coastal Bursts*, reported the departure of various soldiers, who had volunteered for paratroop training. At "Defense B," fewer Fort Miles batteries were kept at Readiness Condition II, however the fort's general defense posture and its formal military routines were observed until war's end in 1945. Very quickly after the war, soldiers were discharged and began going home. The big guns were removed and many of the post's buildings, which had been meticulously maintained and cleaned by GIs under the supervision of sharp-eyed NCOs, were boarded-up. In addition to the American Campaign Medal, all military personnel, who served at Fort Miles during the war, were awarded the World War 2 Victory Medal.

1945: The first Fort Miles soldiers to be discharged joyously depart the post.

---

[61] See Table 2-1

Germany surrendered in May 1945 and Fort Miles' only physical contact with an enemy combatant vessel occurred when the submarine U-858, flying a black flag, was escorted by the US Navy to the fort's mine dock on May 14th. During 1945, Fort Miles was headquarters for German and Italian POW camps scattered throughout Delaware.

In 1946, Fort Miles was briefly the scene of US Navy ramjet tests called *Project Bumblebee*. During the Korean War of the early 1950s, the fort was used for Army training, including live anti-aircraft firing at towed airborne targets. In the late 1950s, many wooden buildings were demolished and the massive concrete casemates converted to administrative and storage space.

Some of the World War 2 underground facilities, such as plotting rooms and ammunition storage "igloos" were buried and remain so today. Some of the artillery spotting towers were used until the 1960s to support radar antennas feeding tracking data to Nike surface-to-air missile batteries protecting Washington and Philadelphia. Ramblers in Cape Henlopen State Park's scrubland can still find discarded artifacts and the remains of abandoned structures.

The Coast Artillery's Last Stand

The advent of anti-ship cruise missiles and air defense surface-to-air missiles, with their very high homing accuracies over much longer ranges, sounded "Taps" for the Coast Artillery's big gun and AAA era. Advanced airborne/spaceborne technologies for ocean and submarine surveillance rapidly obsolesced visual artillery fire control using tall towers, and the Army's Coast Artillery Corps faded quickly into history. Fort Miles' towers, with the exception of the one tower still used by the Delaware Bay and River Pilots, were stripped bare and sealed. Towers #1 and #2, well south of the fort, have suffered from continuous vandalism and unsightly graffiti. The remaining towers are left to age gracefully.

Tower #7, within Henlopen State Park, has been stabilized and equipped with an interior spiral staircase. This tower is open for visitors to climb and enjoy a view that American soldiers once scrutinized with mixed wishes: "Nothing to report" meant continued safety and quiet for a little while longer. Enemy targets within range would at least have meant some action excitement and a chance to get into combat. Decades later, some cannoneers of Fort Miles' World War 2 period wistfully yearned to have had a chance to fight. They must be content, instead, with the certainty that they did their duty, faithfully standing an indispensable watch during a time of sobering uncertainty.

Limited Army Reserve training continued at Fort Miles until the 1980s and some of the old World War 2 barracks buildings close to the beach were converted to R&R furlough quarters for military families stationed throughout the mid-Atlantic area. The Navy operated a portion of its SOSUS Cold War submarine listening system at the fort until it was decommissioned and closed-down in the 1980s.

Epilogue: Cape Henlopen State Park

Even the most casual military history buff can recognize from film documentaries the old German *Küstenartillerie* [62] emplacements on the Normandy coast of France. Key parts of Rommel's *"Atlantic Wall*," the big guns in their reinforced concrete casemates were installed shortly after the fall of France in 1940 but saw very brief action on only a single day: D-Day, June 6, 1944, when they tried unsuccessfully to turn back an Allied invasion known certainly to be coming. Before they were finally silenced or abandoned, however, the guns and their cannoneers were part of a bloody, violent struggle in which the day's outcome was, at times, seriously in doubt.[63]

Across the sea on the US Atlantic seaboard, thinking in synchrony with Rommel's gave rise to the strategic fortification of the East Coast, also starting slowly in 1940. Real concerns that a German naval attack or even invasion from the Atlantic could materialize proved unfounded and the US Coast Artillery Corps saw no domestic combat action during World War 2. But the history buff interested in the German coastal defenses may find it educational and satisfying to clamber over remnant US Coast Artillery emplacements and fire control towers that were critical components of homeland defense during the hardest days of World War 2. These are preserved for close study at Cape Henlopen State Park near Lewes, Delaware.

---

[62] The German Coast Artillery

[63] Winston Churchill, the British PM, was on board HMS Kelvin, a destroyer of the Royal Navy, during the Normandy invasion. Churchill wrote in his memoir, Triumph and Tragedy, "... soon we were within seven to eight thousand yards of the shore. Our [naval] bombardment was leisurely and continuous but there was no reply from the enemy." Churchill refers here to the German *Küstenartillerie*

The State of Delaware acquired Fort Miles from the federal government in 1964 and reopened it as Cape Henlopen State Park. Among the park's many attractions are the surviving remnants of Delaware's role in World War 2, when the state hosted the east coast's most heavily armed military installation. In November 2004, the part of Cape Henlopen State Park that was formerly Fort Miles was added to the National Register of Historic Places. This distinction enhanced efforts to preserve the fort's towers, casemates, and other structures.

Under the stewardship of the late Lee Jennings, Delaware State Park Historian, the Delaware Division of Parks and Recreation teamed with The Fort Miles Historical Association (FMHA) and local history groups to collect and restore World War 2 artifacts for a coast artillery museum in and around the former 12-inch casemate, known as Battery 519. The ambitious vision of FMHA President Dr. Gary Wray, generously supported by benefactors and volunteers, to include what he calls "World War 2 bookends" in the museum has been realized. The "bookends," representing the very first event in the US' role in the war and the very last, are a salvaged piece of the USS Arizona, the first battleship sunk at Pearl Harbor and a 16-in gun from the USS (pictured in Chapter 3).

Almost immediately after the surprise Pearl Harbor attack, parts of the USS Arizona were removed to permit access to parts of the ship where crewmen remained entombed. Removed parts were taken to a dump area within the naval base and lay undisturbed until 1995, when Congress voted to authorize the Navy to distribute them to memorials and museums. The Fort Miles Historical Association acquired a 650-pound steel piece of the aft deck superstructure. At this writing in summer 2021, FMHA was planning to display the Arizona relic in the autumn of 2021 in a museum exhibit called, "Oil Still Bleeds."

Also, the Delaware Seashore Preservation Foundation has partnered with FMHA in the restoration of Fire Control Tower #3, located just south of the town of Dewey Beach, off Route 1 at Tower Road. Following restoration, Tower #3 will be available to visitors for climbing via an interior spiral staircase. The author is supporting the museum's development and the Tower #3 restoration with the proceeds of this book and the reader's purchase is gratefully appreciated.

Reenactors representing 21ˢᵗ Coast Artillery cannoneers of World War 2 practice 6-inch gun drill in the Fort Miles Historic District of Cape Henlopen State Park.

Cape Henlopen State Park is located very near the Lewes, Delaware ferry terminal and is easily reached by car. The park's office can be contacted by telephone at 302-645-8983. The park's main website is at: *http:// www. destateparks.com/chsp/ chsp.htm.* The park office also maintains a Fort Miles oriented website at: *www.fortmiles.org.*	Information about the FMHA and contact information can be found at the association's website: *www.fortmilesha.org.*	DSPF information, an events schedule, and contact details are on its website at *www. savethetower.org* or from PO Box 981, Ocean View, Delaware, 19970; phone: 302-227-2800,.

7

Signature Icons of the Delaware Seashore

State of Delaware tourism ad showing Towers #5 and 6 in a landslide view. These are the same towers pictured on this book's cover.

Logo of the Friends of Cape Henlopen State Park. The Friends maintain an informative website at www.friendsofcapehenlopen.org

This small cement model of a Fort Miles tower stood for many years in the town of Dewey Beach on the east side of Delaware Route 1 at Swedes Street, just north of Towers #3 and #4.

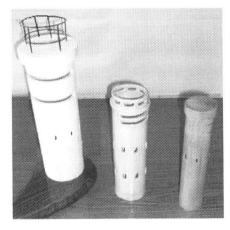

Handcrafted tower mementos available from the FortMiles Historical Association (www.fortmilesha.org).

All proceeds support the development of the Coast Artillery Museum at Cape Henlopen State Park and the restoration of the towers.

Shirts for sale by Bethany Surf Shop on Garfield Parkway near the Boardwalk.

Watercolor miniature by Mike Gala, an architect interested in unusual structures.

106

Laura Hufford's billboard advertising her South Bethany office.

Cover of Delaware Beach Life Magazine

Logo of the Fort Miles Historical Association

Entrance sign to the Tower Shores community, close to Fire Control Tower #3.

Annex A

Other US Coast Defenses in World War 2

Where Fort Miles Fits . . .

In the anxious days leading up to the attack on Pearl Harbor and the frantic scramble to stiffen defenses against feared invasion, the Coast Artillery Corps was charged with two basic missions and was organized accordingly.

Anti-Aircraft Mission. The Corps was responsible for anti-aircraft defenses along all three coasts from Maine to Texas and from Washington State to California. Anti-aircraft units were highly mobile and able to operate from unimproved field positions, often in support of sister units, other military facilities, and civilian areas. Operating independently of their big gun, anti-ship Corps counterparts, the anti-aircraft units provided shoreline coverage against any enemy aircraft seeking to enter US airspace from the sea.

Their armaments ranged from automatic weapons, such as the .50-caliber machine gun pictured above, to cannon capable of firing explosive projectiles at aircraft up to approximately 20,000 feet. Actually comprising the largest number of units in the Coast Artillery Corps and deserving of separate historical recognition, they are not covered further in this discussion. However, it is especially noteworthy that, unlike the big gun batteries, a great many of the Army's anti-aircraft units were deployed overseas intact and resubordinated to European and Pacific Theater commands.

Harbor Defense Mission. The Corps' other main mission was harbor defense and most of the big gun Coast Artillery Regiments and Brigades were designated "HD" as in 21st Coast Artillery Regiment (HD). Mostly operating from fixed positions in fortress-like facilities, the HD batteries were responsible for defending ocean approaches to key US harbors and ports but not every inlet and port was so defended. Furthermore, unlike the anti-aircraft units positioned all along the US shorelines, the Coast Artillery Corps could not provide any anti-ship coverage of very long stretches of the coast. Using the Ft. Miles capabilities as an example, if the Germans had attempted landings on the sandy beaches of Ocean City, Maryland, just 32 miles to the south, none of the fort's big guns could have reached them. Defense of the coastal areas between the fixed HD units was the responsibility of other Army and Navy units.

In World War 2, Harbor defenses were organized by Coast Artillery District (CAD):

- 1st CAD – key New England harbors (see Map A-1)
- 2nd CAD – the port of New York and the Delaware River ports in Pennsylvania, New Jersey, and Delaware (see Map A-2)
- 3rd CAD – Chesapeake Bay entrance to the ports in Virginia, Maryland and Washington DC (see Map A-2)
- 4th CAD – key ports from North Carolina to Texas (see Map A-3)
- 9th CAD – key West Coast ports (see Map A-4)

Additionally, HD capabilities were established outside the Continental US:

- Selected ports in Alaska and Hawaii (see Map A-5)
- Both the Atlantic and Pacific approaches to the Panama Canal (See Map A-6)
- San Juan, Puerto Rico (See Map A-6)
- St John's, Newfoundland (See Map A-6)
- Two key Bermuda ports (See Map A-6)

As the US Navy and Army Air Corps came to grips with both the Japanese and German fleets, pushing them back away from US home waters, the readiness status of the HD units was first relaxed and many were finally stood-down. Many Coast Artillery personnel were shipped overseas to join Field Artillery units, leaving their big fixed-position guns behind.

World War 2: Standard Coast Artillery Equipment

At the onset of America's entry into World War 2, the Coast Artillery was equipped with an assortment of older, frequently obsolete guns – some dating back to the late 19th Century and some which had not been fired for many years. Soon after Pearl Harbor but too late to effect a major change in capabilities at the height of the threat, the Army defined a standard mix of guns for Harbor Defense:

- 16-inch "naval rifles" for use against the longest range targets (up to ~25 miles)
- 6-in guns for targets closer-in (up to ~16 miles)
- 90-mm guns for use against Motor Torpedo Boats (up to ~10 miles).

By the time the critical need for coastal defenses had passed in 1943, few HD units had been upgraded to meet the new standard. By war's end, all the big guns were declared obsolete and no longer manned.

The typical HD unit stationed in the Continental US during the early days of World War 2 operated a similar mix of weapons, sensors, and observation/fire control posts, the latter usually in an elevated structure to gain longer visibility:

- Both large and small-bore anti-ship guns. At some locations, only older 10-inch guns were available; at many locations, mobile 155 mm guns were towed into position and 8-inch guns on railway cars were moved to firing positions on specially-laid track.
- Mines and the support of a mine-planting ship, which may have been home-ported there or may have visited as needed
- Underwater listening devices
- Searchlights
- Primitive radars

Towed 155 mm gun

Although the Coast Artillery had a small variety of the larger fixed guns, their types were standardized and fired common ammunition under common gun drills and procedures. The same was true of the mines, listening devices, searchlights, and the few early radars that were deployed. The significant design differences in the structures used for observation and fire control at various Coast Artillery locations is striking, however.

Other Coast Artillery Towers

The cylindrical towers that remain in Delaware and across the bay at Cape May, New Jersey are unique within the Coast Artillery's history but within that original set of fourteen, no two are exactly alike. Why this is so remains an open question for another researcher to resolve. The eleven towers in Delaware and the remaining[64] two at Cape May, New Jersey are all of different heights, have different numbers of observation slits at different elevations above ground, and all have different window configurations. Nonetheless, they are architecturally pleasing to the eye and have become treasured seascape features to most local residents and visitors.

Following are photos of other surviving World War 2 Coast Artillery observation/fire control towers. All of these remain of historical interest to military history buffs and curious visitors. Many are on state or local park land and under preservation. Except for the two that protected Portsmouth, New Hampshire and the ancient British "Martello" towers, note the general absence of architectural esthetics, which characterize the Delaware and New Jersey towers.

---

[64] Two New Jersey towers at Wildwood and North Wildwood were demolished after World War 2.

*Miller Field, Staten Island,
in New York Harbor*

*Ft. Tilden, New York City
(drawing). This tower was designed
to appear as a lighthouse.*

Wooden tower in Shadmoor State Park, NY

*Adjacent to Montauk
Point Light*

*At Montauk Point, on the eastern tip of Long Island,
protecting the approaches to New York*

An old photo at Halibut Point, Rockport, Massachusetts, Harbor Defenses of Boston.

Ft. Foster, Portsmouth, New Hampshire

Two very unusual examples of "silo" type towers similar to the Delaware and Cape May, New Jersey towers, supporting Harbor Defenses of Portsmouth, NH.

Tower at Cape Elizabeth, Maine

Tower at Pulpit Rock near Rye, New Hampshire

Ft. Dumpling on Conanicut Island, Rhode Island. supporting batteries of Ft Wetherill

Base End Station for Battery Strong, San Diego, California

In Virginia Beach, Virginia: supported both FortStory and Fort Custis

Kodiak, Alaska. A contemporary WWII photo by Roman Salzgiver, stationed there in the 250th CAR

Partridge, New Brunswick, Canada.

Carleton Martello Tower at St. John, New Brunswick, Canada.

Both towers manned in WWII by the 3rd (N.B.) Coast Brigade.

An ancient Martello Tower near Felixstowe, England used for coastal defense in WWII

*German **Kustenartillerie** tower on Alderney, one of the Channel Islands belonging to Great Britain seized after the fall of France, 1940*

116

*Tower supporting Fort
Pickens,Pensacola, Florida*

*Church tower in Colville, Normandy, just
south of Omaha Beach. Used by German
Küstenartillerie as a fire control station during
the D-Day landings.*

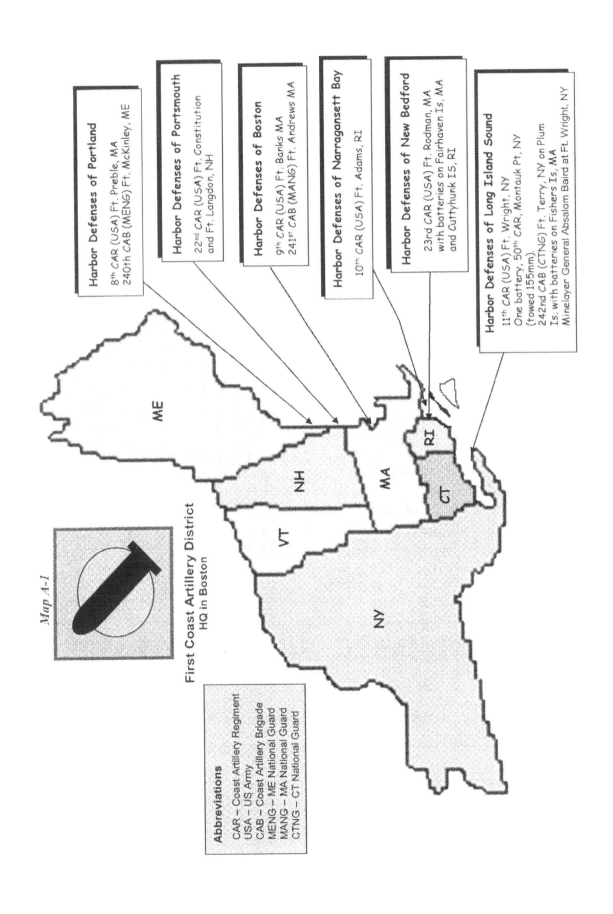

Harbor Defenses of Portland

8th CAR (USA) Ft. Preble, MA
240th CAB (MENG) Ft. McKinley, ME

Harbor Defenses of Portsmouth

22nd CAR (USA) Ft. Constitution
and Ft. Langdon, NH

Harbor Defenses of Boston

9th CAR (USA) Ft. Banks MA
241st CAB (MANG) Ft. Andrews MA

Harbor Defenses of Narragansett Bay

10th CAR (USA) Ft. Adams, RI

Harbor Defenses of New Bedford

23rd CAR (USA) Ft. Rodman, MA
with batteries on Fairhaven Is, MA
and Cuttyhunk IS, RI

Harbor Defenses of Long Island Sound

11th CAR (USA) Ft. Wright, NY
One battery, 50th CAR, Montauk Pt, NY
(towed 155mm).
242nd CAB (CTNG) Ft. Terry, NY on Plum
Is. with batteries on Fishers Is, MA
Minelayer General Absalom Baird at Ft. Wright, NY

Map A-1

First Coast Artillery District
HQ in Boston

ME

NH

VT

MA

RI

CT

NY

Abbreviations

CAR – Coast Artillery Regiment
USA – US Army
CAB – Coast Artillery Brigade
MENG – ME National Guard
MANG – MA National Guard
CTNG – CT National Guard

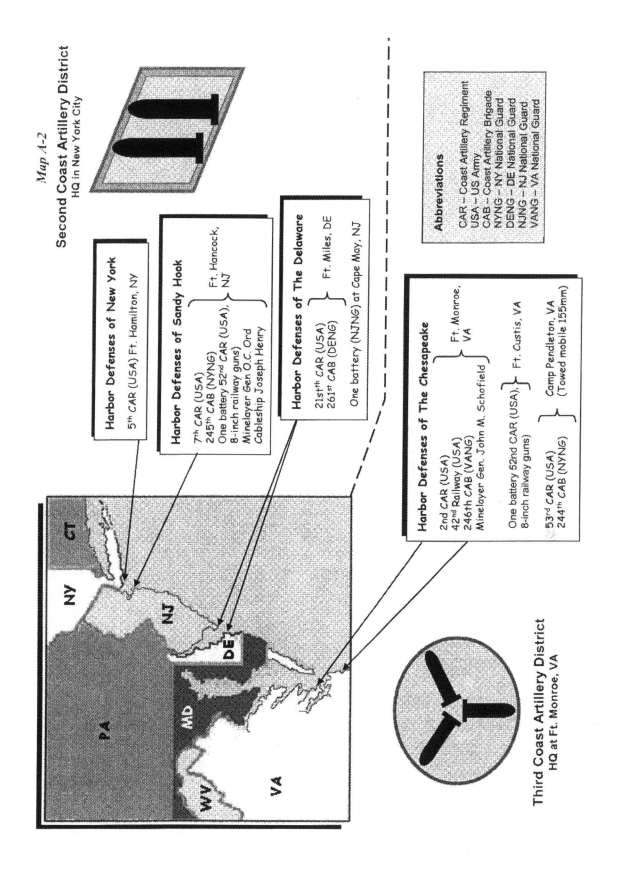

Map A-2

Second Coast Artillery District
HQ in New York City

Harbor Defenses of New York
5th CAR (USA) Ft. Hamilton, NY

Harbor Defenses of Sandy Hook
{ Ft. Hancock, NJ
7th CAR (USA)
245th CAB (NYNG)
One battery 52nd CAR (USA),
8-inch railway guns)
Minelayer Gen O.C. Ord
Cableship Joseph Henry

Harbor Defenses of The Delaware
{ Ft. Miles, DE
21st th CAR (USA)
261st CAB (DENG)
One battery (NJNG) at Cape May, NJ

Harbor Defenses of The Chesapeake
{ Ft. Monroe, VA
2nd CAR (USA)
42nd Railway (USA)
246th CAB (VANG)
Minelayer Gen. John M. Schofield
{ Ft. Custis, VA
One battery 52nd CAR (USA),
8-inch railway guns)
{ Camp Pendleton, VA
(Towed mobile 155mm)
53rd CAR (USA)
244th CAB (NYNG)

Abbreviations
CAR – Coast Artillery Regiment
USA – US Army
CAB – Coast Artillery Brigade
NYNG – NY National Guard
DENG – DE National Guard
NJNG – NJ National Guard
VANG – VA National Guard

Third Coast Artillery District
HQ at Ft. Monroe, VA

119

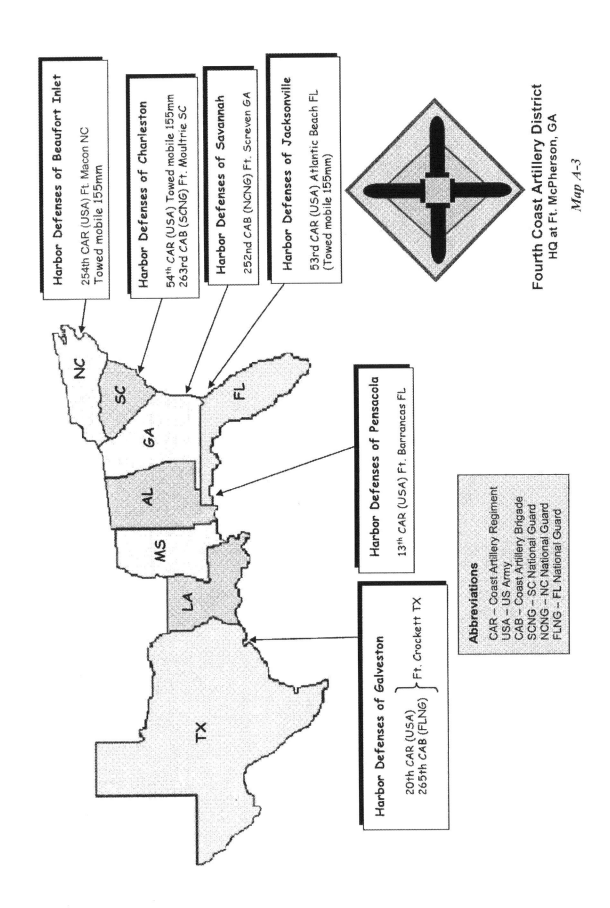

Harbor Defenses of Beaufort Inlet

254th CAR (USA) Ft. Macon NC
Towed mobile 155mm

Harbor Defenses of Charleston

54th CAR (USA) Towed mobile 155mm
263rd CAB (SCNG) Ft. Moultrie SC

Harbor Defenses of Savannah

252nd CAB (NCNG) Ft. Screven GA

Harbor Defenses of Jacksonville

53rd CAR (USA) Atlantic Beach FL
(Towed mobile 155mm)

Harbor Defenses of Pensacola

13th CAR (USA) Ft. Barrancas FL

Harbor Defenses of Galveston

20th CAR (USA)
265th CAB (FLNG) } Ft. Crockett TX

Fourth Coast Artillery District
HQ at Ft. McPherson, GA

Map A-3

Abbreviations

CAR – Coast Artillery Regiment
USA – US Army
CAB – Coast Artillery Brigade
SCNG – SC National Guard
NCNG – NC National Guard
FLNG – FL National Guard

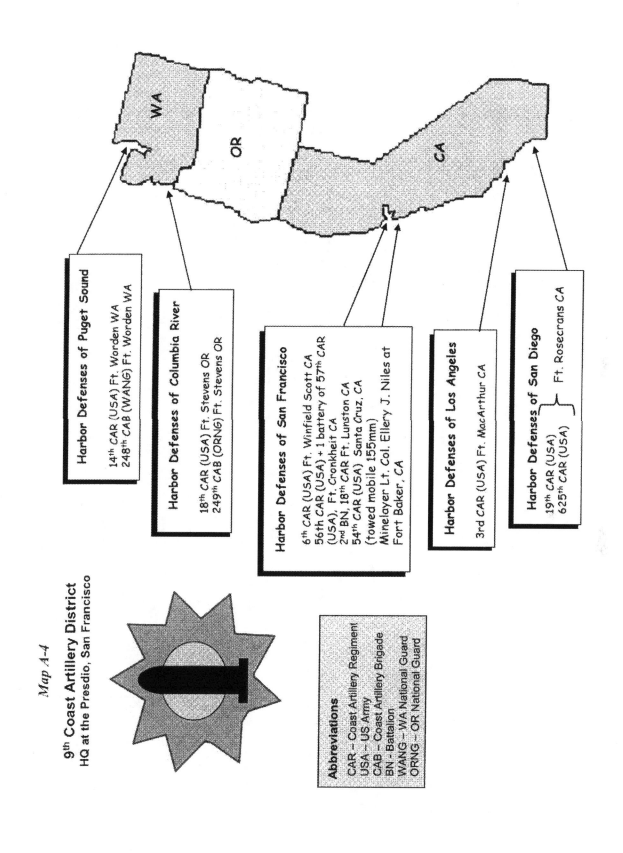

Map A-4

9th Coast Artillery District
HQ at the Presdio, San Francisco

Harbor Defenses of Puget Sound

14th CAR (USA) Ft. Worden WA
248th CAB (WANG) Ft. Worden WA

Harbor Defenses of Columbia River

18th CAR (USA) Ft. Stevens OR
249th CAB (ORNG) Ft. Stevens OR

Harbor Defenses of San Francisco

6th CAR (USA) Ft. Winfield Scott CA
56th CAR (USA) + 1 battery of 57th CAR
(USA), Ft. Cronkheit CA
2nd BN, 18th CAR Ft. Lunston CA
54th CAR (USA) Santa Cruz, CA
(towed mobile 155mm)
Minelayer Lt. Col. Ellery J. Niles at
Fort Baker, CA

Harbor Defenses of Los Angeles

3rd CAR (USA) Ft. MacArthur CA

Harbor Defenses of San Diego

19th CAR (USA)   ⎤
625th CAR (USA)   ⎦ Ft. Rosecrans CA

Abbreviations

CAR – Coast Artillery Regiment
USA – US Army
CAB – Coast Artillery Brigade
BN – Battalion
WANG – WA National Guard
ORNG – OR National Guard

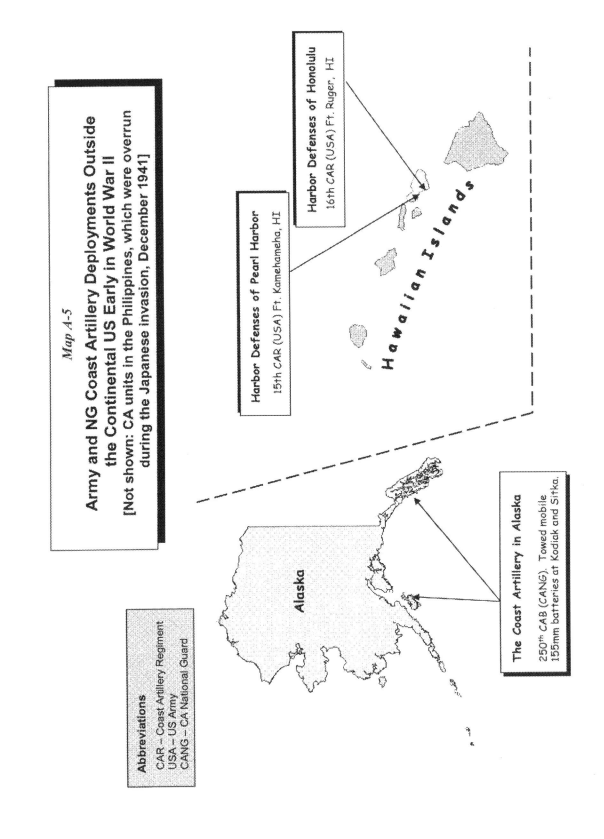

Map A-5

Army and NG Coast Artillery Deployments Outside the Continental US Early in World War II

[Not shown: CA units in the Philippines, which were overrun during the Japanese invasion, December 1941]

Harbor Defenses of Honolulu
16th CAR (USA) Ft. Ruger, HI

Harbor Defenses of Pearl Harbor
15th CAR (USA) Ft. Kamehameha, HI

Hawaiian Islands

Alaska

The Coast Artillery in Alaska
250th CAB (CANG). Towed mobile 155mm batteries at Kodiak and Sitka.

Abbreviations
CAR – Coast Artillery Regiment
USA – US Army
CANG – CA National Guard

122

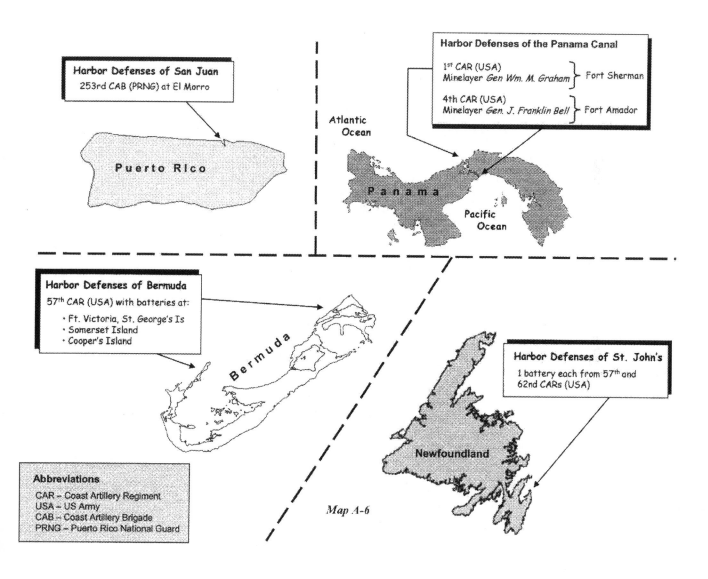

Harbor Defenses of San Juan
253rd CAB (PRNG) at El Morro

Puerto Rico

Atlantic Ocean

Harbor Defenses of the Panama Canal

1st CAR (USA)
Minelayer *Gen Wm. M. Graham* } Fort Sherman

4th CAR (USA)
Minelayer *Gen. J. Franklin Bell* } Fort Amador

P a n a m a

Pacific Ocean

Harbor Defenses of Bermuda
57th CAR (USA) with batteries at:
• Ft. Victoria, St. George's Is
• Somerset Island
• Cooper's Island

B e r m u d a

Harbor Defenses of St. John's
1 battery each from 57th and 62nd CARs (USA)

Newfoundland

Map A-6

Abbreviations
CAR – Coast Artillery Regiment
USA – US Army
CAB – Coast Artillery Brigade
PRNG – Puerto Rico National Guard

123

Annex B

Defense of the Delaware Searchlight Plan

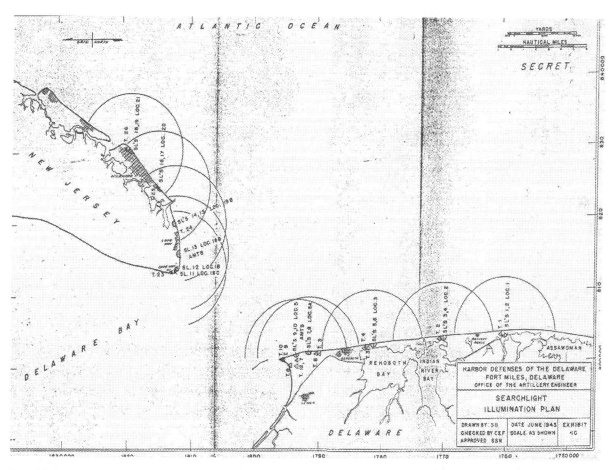

Searchlight Plan for Delaware and New Jersey batteries at the end of World War 2 (June 1945). The plan was classified Secret. Note that the plan depicts overlapping illumination along the New Jersey and Delaware shorelines covered by the Coast Artillery guns but does not provide coverage for a ship entering Delaware Bay in the middle of the main channel.

Annex C

Computing the "Flight Time" of
an Artillery Projectile

As has been stressed in several places in *Delaware's Ghost Towers*, the combat effectiveness of a World War 2 Coast Artillery battery would have depended primarily on the battery's ability to predict where a moving target was going to be at a specific point in time and then to fire projectiles that would arrive at that spot at the same time the target did. "Plot Forward" lead times were routinely factored into all firing solutions. The faster the target was moving and the more varied its evasive maneuvering, the more complicated the firing solution became.

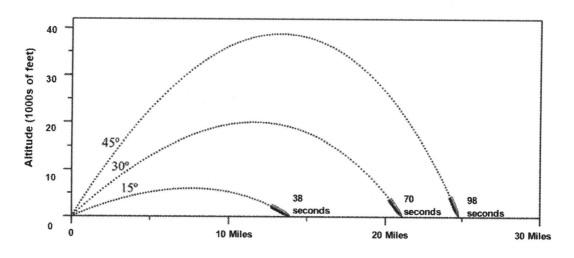

Distance from gun to target
[16-inch projectile, 2700 fps muzzle velocity]

Graph by Professor Dean R. Wheeler,
Brigham Young University

127

Annex D

Two guesses at what might have happened

Until this point in *Delaware's Ghost Towers*, all of the text has been strictly historical. Annex D, consisting of an Annex D-1 and an Annex D-2, offers Alternative History or *"What If"* conjectures using the actual historical background as a framework.

Annex D-1

December 1941: A German Attack on Wilmington

What might have been - a fictitious, hypothetical "Alternative History" scenario . . .

Suppose the German admiral of its submarine fleet seized the moment of the German declaration of War against the US right after the Japanese attack on Pearl Harbor to "get even" for perceived American interference with U-Boat operations in the Atlantic?

During all of 1941, *Großadmiral* Erich Räder, in command of the German *Kriegsmarine*,[65] had chafed under the restrictive Rules of Engagement forced on him by what he saw as the sham of American neutrality. The frustrated Grand Admiral risked admonishing Hitler in blunt terms that German naval forces would "if need be, resort to arms" if American warships should try "to prevent them from exercising their right" to sink enemy merchant ships." Räder also complained bitterly about American ocean patrols and hinted that Americans' communicating the positions of German naval units to the Royal Navy should be treated as acts of war.[66] He ached to shake off what he felt were the unnecessarily timid rules and to settle scores with the Americans.

At last, Räder's spirits soared with news of the December 7th Japanese attack on Pearl Harbor and Germany's Declaration of War on the US on December 11th. Räder impulsively decided to begin his long-delayed operations against America with a raid that replicated the *Kriegsmarine's* preemptive attack inside Danzig harbor at the start of Germany's invasion of Poland, two years earlier.[67] On his own authority, he directed his senior operations staff to plan a symbolic strike at a strategic target on the US mainland at the earliest practical date.

Großadmiral
Erich Räder

Räder christened the initiative himself: *Unternehmen Frechheit* (Operation Audacity).

---

[65] Navy

[66] *http://www.nationarchive.com/Summaries/v152i0022_03.htm.*

[67] September 1, 1939. (See the discussion in Chapter 1).

Faced with a truly difficult cross-ocean operational and logistical challenge, and mindful of their need to husband fleet resources against the suddenly magnified threat posed by the US Navy, the staff planners immediately ruled out any "suicide" missions. They were also hobbled by the unavailability of any spare combatant vessels not already assigned to ongoing operations. After secret intelligence briefings about US port defenses, the most desirable but also most heavily-defended targets, New York City and Washington, DC, were reluctantly taken off the list.

The oil refineries and storage tanks, chemical plants, and seagoing tankers tied up at Wilmington, Delaware, however, were obviously valuable strategic targets and Wilmington was accordingly proposed to the *Großadmiral* for his approval. Räder liked the idea and scrawled his concurrence at the top of the cover page with the exhortation, *Sobald möglich!!*[68]

The early preferred choice of a raid by fast E-Boats[69] was quickly abandoned because their short ranges would require too many at-sea refuelings crossing the Atlantic and their firepower was too limited. The planners settled instead on fleet destroyers and requested that Räder detach two of them for *Frechheit.* He was not refused by his intimidated task force commander at St. Nazaire in occupied France, who released the two vessels and complained only in his personal diary. At the planning conference at headquarters, the skippers of Destroyers Z8/Heinemann and Z20/Galster, received their *Segelnbefehl*[70] stamped *Streng Geheim*[71] on each page. Z8's *Korvettenkapitän* Karl Alberts was named the task section commander. Alberts was thrilled by his selection and eagerly looked forward to the chance to distinguish himself, away from his unexciting escort assignments.

---

[68] As soon as possible!!
[69] Motor Torpedo Boats
[70] Sailing Order
[71] Top Secret

Destroyers Z8 and Z20 head west from the French Coast

The key elements of the *Frecheit* plan provided:

Navigation

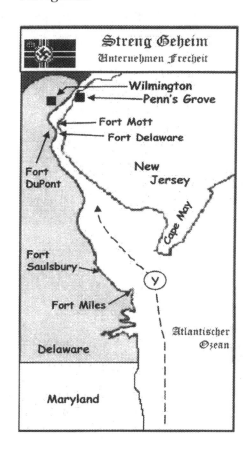

- Westbound Atlantic crossing arriving at *Punkt Gustav*[72], latitude 37°-30' 60 kilometres[73] off Parramore Island, Virginia. Commence trail formation with Z8 leading Z20 by 1 kilometre. Steam parallel to and 60 kilometres from enemy coast to *Punkt Ypsilon*.[74]

- To take advantage of the new moon and dark night sky, Z8 and Z20 will enter Delaware Bay from *Punkt Ypsilon* at sunset, 1641 hours (4:41pm), US Eastern Time on 17 December 1941.

- According to most current US-based intelligence sources, defensive blackouts are not in force.[75] Delaware River and Bay lighthouses and channel markers are still lit at night and are expected to be available for navigating the bay and river.[76] Ships'

---

[72] Point G

[73] 37.5 miles

[74] Point Y

[75] Factual. Blackouts were not observed and "dim-outs" – a partial measure – were not imposed until May of 1942.

[76] Factual. German U-Boats actually navigated the US east coast by using lighthouses still operating through all of 1941.

bridge parties will also be able to steer by town street lights and other lights ashore not subject to blackout.

- Sail at 37 kph in the main shipping channel, steaming 110 kilometres[77] up the Delaware River for 3 hours.

- Estimated Time of Arrival at Wilmington harbor just after 1940 hours (7:41 pm).

- Commence firing immediately. Expend all 12.7cm and 3.7mm ammunition. Remain in the Wilmington target operations area no longer than 20 minutes.

- At best speed, retrace the ingress route down the Delaware River into Delaware Bay and out into the ocean before sunrise at 0720 hours. Once in Delaware Bay, begin evasive maneuvering and continue until *Punkt Siegfried* [78] 40 kilometres east of Cape Henlopen, Delaware.

- Return to base at St. Nazaire at best speed.

Logistics

- Both destroyers would depart St. Nazaire with full fuel tanks plus extended range auxiliary tanks.

- 120% of normal ammunition loads would be embarked. Between the two destroyers, armaments consisted of:
  - ten 12.7cm guns
  - twenty-eight 37mm rapid-fire guns firing explosive rounds
  - fourteen 20mm heavy machine guns
  - sixteen torpedo tubes with a total of sixty-four torpedoes
  - one hundred twenty mines
  - eighty-four standard-issue rifles
  - ten submachine guns

- West-bound and east-bound at-sea refuelings by fleet tanker at positions to be determined.

---

[77] ~69 miles

[78] Point S

Combat Operations

- Immediately clear of St. Nazaire, ships will be totally blacked-out except for subdued red stern lamp visible by ship following closely in trail. Ships will communicate with each other only by flags and signal lamp.

- Refueling tankers will transmit encoded rendezvous positions; destroyers will maintain radio silence and will not acknowledge.

- Ships' crews will go to and remain at Battle Stations when *Punkt Gustav*[79] (60 kilometres off the US coast) has been reached. All armaments will be manned, loaded and ready.

- During northbound ingress, Z8 and Z20 will pass three key danger zones:

  - Fort Miles at the mouth of Delaware Bay with four 155mm guns on the western shore and two 155mm guns at Cape May in New Jersey. Both sites may have searchlights.

  - Fort Saulsbury just east of Milford, Delaware, inside Delaware Bay. The fort has four 12-inch guns and may have searchlights.

  - At Delaware City, in a narrow part of the river, there are three defensive forts with heavy guns to be passed and all may have searchlights (Fort Dupont on the western shore; Fort Delaware on Peapatch Island in the river; and Fort Mott on the eastern shore in New Jersey).

- When approaching enemy defensive forts, all active searchlights will be brought under fire and neutralized by ships' 37mm and 20mm guns. All observed personnel and vehicle movements in these areas should also be brought under fire.

- As soon as Wilmington oil refineries with nearby storage tanks and DuPont Chemical Works across the river at Penn's Grove, New Jersey come within range of the ships' main 5-inch mounts, commence rapid, sustained firing.

- All torpedoes should be launched at enemy vessels moored at Wilmington and Penn's Grove docks and anchorages. Expend all torpedoes. Tankers, freighters, and Navy/Coast Guard combatants should be prioritized.

- After 20 minutes in the target area, Z8 and Z20 immediately begin to withdraw at best speed.

---

[79] Point G

- Mine laying:

  - One-half of mine stocks on board should be laid in the river between Wilmington and Delaware City.

  - One-quarter of mine stocks on board should be laid in the bend of the river off Bay View Beach, Delaware.

  - Remaining mine stocks should be laid in the river between Woodland Beach, Delaware and Gandy's Beach, New Jersey

- During egress, ships' bridge parties must watch for enemy attempts to block downriver progress. Evasive maneuvers, as possible, and engagement with remaining available armaments may be required.

Communications

- Z8 and Z20 are to maintain 24-hour radio watch on *Kriegsmarine Hohefrequenz Befehlsendung*.[80] The mission abort codeword is *Aufzug* [81] plus authenticator codegroup appropriate for date of transmission.

- Break radio silence if engaged by enemy vessels while at sea or if reconnoitered by enemy aircraft.

- Z8: send encrypted damage assessment codeword, as appropriate, on 3755 and 5420 KHz[82] on reaching *Punkt Siegfried* during egress.

Intelligence and Special Operations Support

- A *Funkaufklarungsdienst* [83] section will be embarked in Z8. Section will monitor and analyze enemy tactical communications to detect reactions to Z8 and Z20 movements. Section also has English-language capabilities to intrude false information and commands into enemy radio nets and can also jam selected frequencies.

---

[80] Navy High Frequency Command Broadcast
[81] A randomly-selected codeword (Elevator), whose meaning does not pertain to the action
[82] Kz = German for "*kilozyklen*" or kilocycles. Has been replaced by "kilohertz," abbreviated "KHz"
[83] Radio Intelligence Service

- Planned Special Operations support was briefed to the two destroyer captains but was not published in the order.

  - Captains of both destroyers were briefed immediately to repeat back any challenges flashed at them by signal lamps on enemy ships or aircraft. Intelligence had advised that this ruse had sometimes caused enemy signalmen to flash back the response that was expected to their challenge.

  - On the afternoon of December 17, *Gestapo* operatives in the US (actually members of the German-American *Bund* but not identified as such) would detonate a large truck-bomb in a rail yard outside the Philadelphia suburb of Chester, northeast of Wilmington. The objective would be setting afire rail tank cars and distracting the attention of area fire brigades and emergency crews.

  - At 1505 hours (3:05pm), US Eastern Time, a designated U-Boat will masquerade as a US merchantman and transmit a decoy "Submarine Sighted" signal ("SSS") on the US Navy/Coast Guard watch net. The false sighting position report off Barnegat Light, New Jersey has objective of drawing enemy patrols away from the mouth of Delaware Bay.

December 17, 1941: Hypothetical Events

After an Atlantic crossing between latitudes 35 and 37 degrees, two uneventful mid-ocean refuelings, and giving Bermuda wide berth, Z8 and Z20 arrived at *Punkt Gustav* just after noon on December 17th. During the four-day crossing, only two smoke smudges on the distant horizon were spotted and, on the evening of the 16th, one unidentified aircraft was seen a long way off in the western sky. It did not approach and the Germans were not challenged. Both destroyers sounded "General Quarters" and 574 excited German crewmen ran to battle stations on the two ships, beginning their strained, anxious watch for the enemy.

The eastern sky had begun graying at 0650 (6:50am) but heavy low clouds would block the sun all day. *Korvettenkapitän* Alberts shaped a curved course that kept them out of sight of land and ate up time until their planned turn at 1641 hours (4:41pm). As the two raiders approached *Punkt Ypsilon*, a cold wind was up, blowing strongly from the southwest and pushing 10-foot waves that rolled the German ships uncomfortably. At 1506 hours, Z8's *Funkaufklarungsdienst* cell reported that an "SSS" call was sent three times by a callsign PTJH and that a US Navy station was trying to reach PTJH with no response. Between 1520 and 1550 hours, the cell copied first station COAST GUARD RESCUE ONE and then station MIKE ROGER SIX calling the non-existent ship in peril.

The wind was audible and snow was blowing sideways from a sky the same shade of near-black as the sea with no horizon when *Leutnant* Kalbeck, the lead navigator on Z8, shouted his estimate that they had arrived at their turning point and a very tense but trusting Alberts ordered the course change. Nonetheless, the German skipper tightly gripped the rail under the forward glass of the bridge, steadying himself as he anxiously searched the darkness for some confirmation that they had entered the mouth of the bay. The stern lookout reported that their companion, Z20, was in trail, right behind.

Albert's first sight of America, the Harbor of Refuge Light just inside Delaware Bay, caught him by surprise off the port bow and his first impulse was to keep quiet lest his voice give away their position. But first one lookout then several on the ship's port side sang out. They were inside the bay but without any sight of land. A broadly grinning Alberts looked across at Kalbeck and spoke enthusiastically for all to hear, "*Großer Mann!*"[84]. After an apprehensive full minute of barreling ahead at their rolling 20-knot clip, a lookout in the bow of Z8 spotted an illuminated channel marker and Alberts ordered a slight correction to starboard. No searchlights began to probe for them from Cape Henlopen or Cape May. The two German destroyers were running for Wilmington, right on course, right on schedule.

---

[84] Great Man

Annex D-2

Provocative Cruise Of The Iron Fleet

Only a couple of momentous, far-reaching decisions could have completely changed the course of World War 2 and the world we live in now.

Imagine a plausible scenario in which the Japanese attack at Pearl Harbor had been continued as originally planned, with successive waves of bomb and torpedo strikes until almost all US ships had been put out of action and the fuel stores and repair facilities had been destroyed. In such a scenario, further consider the possibility that, without its Pacific Fleet, the US dared not declare war on Japan, instead feeling weak and backing off to give Japan a free hand in Asia. Further imagine that Churchill yielded to fellow cabinet members fearful of a rapacious German invasion and that Britain had sued for peace after its army had been defeated and captured at Dunkirk. Lastly, let's assume that Franklin D. Roosevelt had chosen not to seek a fourth term and was succeeded in 1941 by President Norman Thomas and also that Winston Churchill was replaced by Clement Atlee as Prime Minister.

With Japan and Germany triumphant across the seas from the US and Canada, might Germany have used pressures and intimidation to coerce economic and political concessions from a new and untested US presidential administration?

What might have been - a fictitious, hypothetical "Alternative History" scenario . .

The decoded incoming cable marked 'FLASH" from the Royal Canadian Navy base at St. John's, Newfoundland started young sailors in whites flat-out running the halls in US Navy Headquarters in Washington. In the 1940s days before copiers, office automation and local area networks, teletype machines were loaded with 5-ply papers separated by carbon paper. The original, rubber-stamped "SECRET" in red ink, and the top three carbon copies of the Canadian message were rushed by the runners to the offices of the Chief of Naval Operations and three of his senior deputies. The

Communications Center immediately started printing additional copies from the punched-paper tape that had been created when the message was decoded.

Admiral Ernest King

In the CNO's office, Commander John Crowley, the CNO's aide, skimmed the message and took it right in to Admiral Ernest King. King read the text twice and told Crowley to ask the Battle Staff to assemble in the Command Center. King then wrote the names of others on the message, including the President's naval aide, who should see the message and handed the yellow paper to a WAVE yeoman before heading to the Command Center himself. By the time Admiral King reached the Command Center, a copy of the Canadian message had been read by the staff and the Senior Watch Officer had the giant wall map of the World tagged with the last-known position of the *Kriegsmarine's* fearsome *Atlantische Eisenflotte*.[85]

Amid lavish ceremonial fanfare accented by brass bands, flowers and bunting, dignitaries in formal dress, bellowing ships' horns, and smartly-dressed crews at attention on all the decks, the Iron Atlantic Fleet, champions of German sea power, had made a striking departure from Kiel harbor on April 9, 1945, captured by the world's photojournalists and newsreel photographers. 500 *Luftwaffe* bombers in *staffel* formations overflew the departing ships at an altitude of 100 meters,[86] creating a vibrating roar on the ground that affected the balance of many standing onlookers.

The *Führer* himself conceived the naval show of force and attended the ceremony, watching from the yacht *Sachsenhausen* and had to cover his ears as the bombers thundered overhead. Hitler's model was the 1907 world tour of America's Great White Fleet. The

Bismarck

---

[85] Atlantic Iron Fleet

[86] Approximately 300 feet

principal audience for the tour of *Die Große Eisenflotte*[87] was recently-inaugurated President Norman Thomas.

From Kiel, the naval giants *Bismarck* and *Tirpitz*, accompanied by heavy cruisers *Scharnhorst*, *Graf Spee*, *Deutschland*, *Gniesenau*, and Prinz *Eugen*, plus fifteen destroyers and fleet support vessels visited: occupied Copenhagen and Stavanger, Norway; Bruges, Belgium; Rotterdam; and Le Havre.

Prime Minister Clement Atlee apologized to an irate and adamantly opposed King George VI and then advised a nonplussed Commons that the Cabinet had approved a 48-hour "good will" visit by the German ships to Plymouth. Black crepe, usually reserved for mourning displays, hung from the windows of many English homes to signal that the German presence was a bitter pill to swallow. However, the people of Plymouth, traditionally a Royal Navy town, and the German crews ashore on leave behaved politely and German money was gratefully accepted by pub landlords, shopkeepers, tattoo artists, and opportunistic "good time" girls.

At the conclusion of the German visit on April 22nd, Admiral Günther Lütjens, in *Bismarck*, ordered each ship in the formation to fire a one-shot salvo from each of its main guns in salute as the fleet got underway from Plymouth. Although the guns were all pointed out to sea, the powerful concussions broke windows, set pigeons flying, and made young children cry.

Before the smoke had cleared, over 200 Luftwaffe bombers based in Northern France and the Channel Islands roared over the harbor and the departing ships at very low altitude. Adult Britons cringed in memory of the 1940 wartime bombings and ruefully looked around at the ruins that still littered some Plymouth streets, muttering anti-*Nazi* oaths to themselves.

Lütjens next headed for bunkering and provisions at St. Nazaire on France's Atlantic Coast and then steamed to the Azores, putting in at the port of *Angrodo do Héroismo* on the island of Terceira. Three days later, on April 30th, the sunrise revealed the Germans suddenly gone and US naval intelligence had suspicions but no hard sightings or radio intercepts that revealed where the fleet had headed or if it were still intact.

---

[87] The Great Iron Fleet

After a further two days without any intelligence suggesting that the Germans had sailed back to Europe, there were many American high-placed hunches that Lütjens was either heading for the *Kriegsmarine* base at *Sankt Peter*, off Canada, or the Caribbean and South America.

Admiral Günther Lütjens

The German bases in Greenland, *"Ankerplatz Eisbär"* and *"Logistikbasis Edelweis"* were still locked-in by winter ice and assessed as improbable ports-of-call. The Secretary of the Navy directed that no information be released that would alarm the general public or reveal that the US was only guessing at where the German might be heading.

Short Mark III Sunderland

Early on May 4th, a *Sunderland* flying boat of the Canadian Maritime Patrol spotted the fleet heading for the island of *Sankt Peter*, south of Newfoundland. The tiny port offered insufficient anchorage for the whole fleet so only *Bismarck* and the destroyer Z17 *Von Roeder* were berthed while the rest of the fleet bobbed offshore.

At dawn on May 8th, a Canadian fishing crew out of Sydney, Nova Scotia stared in disbelief as the fog-colored German seagoing giants materialized out of the drizzle, heading southwest towards New England. The fishermen, trembling in fearful anticipation of being blown out of the water, still dutifully contacted the Canadian Coast Guard, which made a report by radiotelephone to the Navy in St. John's that formed the basis of the coded cable that was flashed to Washington:

GERMAN FLEET SIGHTED 081030Z[88] NORTH OF SABLE ISLAND NS HEADING SOUTHWEST.

Within the hour, dozens of additional sighting reports came in, originating from freighters, ferries and aircraft. For the remaining daylight hours, sighting reports totaled in the hundreds, although the accuracy of numbers and types of ships varied widely, with some reports erroneously claiming to have sighted German aircraft carriers. CBC Toronto was first on the air with broadcast bulletins, quickly echoed by US networks and the threatening German fleet was the subject of huge headlines in all US newspapers. The American public was agitated and stirred to great anxiety by hyped predictions offered by the leading radio news commentators. The US Navy's Atlantic Fleet went on maximum alert and positioned all available combatant ships along the East Coast right on the edge of the three-mile territorial limit but with strict orders to stay within home waters.

When the lead destroyer, of the German formation, the Z16 *Friedrich Eckoldt*, blinked her position as 125 kilometers off Nantucket Island, Lütjens ordered the whole fleet to Battle Stations, in keeping with his sailing orders. At breakfast aboard *Bismarck* before going ashore in Kiel, Grand Admiral Eric Räder had wished Lütjens a happy voyage, lamented that he could not participate in so historic a German accomplishment, and putting on his uniform cap, soberly reviewed the fleet's sailing order, documenting his specific rules of engagement with the Americans:

Segelnbefehl [89]

- The fleet was to very conservatively observe the US' claimed 4.8 kilometer[90] territorial limit by coming no closer than 25 kilometers[91] to any US land.
- No fleet vessel was permitted any courtesy visits in US ports, even if invited, and Lütjens was to handle any emergencies and maintenance difficulties within his own resources.

---

[88] 6:30am Atlantic Time on the 8th
[89] Sailing Order
[90] 4.8 kilometers = 3 miles
[91] 25 kilometers = almost 16 miles

- The fleet's accompanying screen was to position destroyers between the fleet's main combatants and any US Navy or Coast Guard vessel that approached, permitting no American approaches closer than 4 kilometers.[92]

- The fleet was to maintain scout plane reconnaissance during all daylight hours. Scout planes were to avoid closer contact than 4 kilometers with any US aircraft and ships.

- Crews of all ships were to remain at Battle Stations when the fleet was within 100 kilometers[93] of any US territory. While at Battle Stations, the fleet was to be blacked-out and to observe ship-to-ship radio silence, communicating only by flag hoists or signaling lamps. During ship-to-ship radio silence, only *Bismarck* was permitted to report the fleet's position daily at midnight and noon via *Enigma*-encrypted High Frequency radio to the communications station, VB-51, on *Sankt Peter* for relay to Berlin.

- The fleet would be provided tactical Communications Intelligence support by the *B-Dienst*[94] detachment embarked in *Scharnhorst*. Upon the detected flight of any American aircraft, all radars other than air surveillance sets were to be shut down.

- If need be, Lütjens was authorized to resort to arms if American warships should try to prevent the fleet from exercising their right of way in international waters. "Keep Away" warnings by flag hoists or signaling lamps should be given first, followed by warning shots across the bow, before any firing for effect. Fleet vessels were always authorized to return fire, if fired upon.

- Expected hostile American action was to be reported with the codeword, "*weizenmehl.*"[95] sent three times. In the event of actual hostilities, radio silence was to be broken and reports radioed to *Sankt Peter* and Berlin in plaintext.

---

[92] 4 kilometers = 2.5 miles
[93] 100 kilometers = 80 miles
[94] *Beobachtungsdienst,* German Navy Communications Intelligence Service
[95] A randomly-selected codeword (wheatflour), whose meaning does not pertain to the action

The Iron Fleet Off the US Coast

At 1512 hours Eastern Standard Time, Destroyer Z16 reported her arrival at *Punkt Gustav*,[96] on latitude 40 degrees, 25 kilometers off New York City, and the fleet changed course, steering 225 degrees and slowed to ten knots, maintaining a 25-

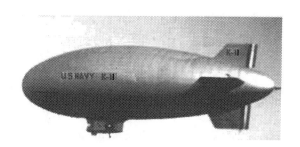

mile offshore track. The turn was reported by the crew of the US Navy blimp, K-11, out of Lakehurst Naval Air Station, New Jersey. K-11, flown by Lieutenant (Jg) Frank Lunney, was a long-endurance reconnaissance platform, and was inching ever closer to the German fleet to photograph individual ships in as much detail as possible.

When Lütjens felt K-11 was crowding too closely, he ordered *Bismarck* and *Tirpitz* each to launch an *Arado* Ar 196 floatplane from their on-board catapults. The two *Arados* intercepted the blimp and *Leutnant* Erich Baumgartner, flying the lead plane, fired warning shots from its twin 20mm machine guns. Lt. Lunney watched the tracer rounds zipping closely by and immediately turned toward shore, disappointing Baumgartner, who was hoping for orders to shoot the blimp down. Lakehurst Operations ordered Lunney to approach no closer than ten miles but to climb to 6000 feet and continue pacing the Germans.

Later the same day, the aircraft carrier USS Ranger (CV-4) launched a section of twelve Hellcat fighters while just off Virginia Beach. Under orders to approach no closer than five miles from the

Arado Ar 196

German ships, the Hellcats were picked up first by destroyer Z16's radar and signaled by blinker lamp throughout the fleet.

Bismarck and *Tirpitz* again launched their *Arado* Ar 196s, which approached and flew parallel to the blue fighters but stayed well outside the prohibited 16-mile buffer. Baumgartner was aloft again but soberly watched the twelve blue Hellcats, feeling no strong desire to engage them in his low-performance float plane.

---

[96] Point "G" in the German phonetic alphabet

Newspapers in Germany and Japan published front-page photos of the small *Arados* apparently barring the American fighters from approaching the fleet and accompanying captions poked fun at the US' feeble response. Days later, photo reprints, complete with the *Nazi* captions, appeared in American papers, bringing embarrassment to the Thomas Administration and to the Navy in particular.

The First Army Headquarters Command Post at Fort Jay, New York, was monitoring intelligence on the German fleet's movements and plotting successively reported positions on a large plexiglass map. With no troop transports sighted, the Army's intelligence assessment was that the probability of invasion was low and, while First Army's infantry and armored divisions were placed on RED Alert, they were all kept in garrison. Army Air Forces bomber units were loaded for anti-ship missions and all their crews were recalled to bases.

Based on blimp K-11's reports, the Germans were estimated to be 16 miles off-shore, well within the 22-mile range of the battleships' 15-inchers and the cruisers' 11 inchers. The fleet's combined main armament brought to bear sixteen 15-inch and thirty-six 11-inch guns that could easily reach US targets on shore. Leaves and passes for all Coast Artillerymen were cancelled and batteries along the Atlantic seaboard were placed at Readiness Condition I but ordered not to open fire without direct authorization to do so from 2nd Coast Artillery District at Fort Totten, New York. However, once the Germans had sailed below the 40th parallel, the readiness of the cannoneers in New York and New England was lowered but no leaves or passes were allowed.

Colonel George Ruhlen, commanding the 21st Coast Artillery Regiment at Fort Miles, Delaware had his main batteries manned and ready with powder and armor-piercing projectiles loaded for near-maximum range. All of his regiment's SCR-296 radars were scanning the ocean approaches to Delaware Bay all the way south to the Maryland line. At night, the searchlight batteries at water's edge kept their generators running continuously as they themselves tried to escape the cold on-shore winds and blowing sand. Artillery fire controllers were in-place in their towers, just behind the beach, searching the horizon for German ships with binoculars and azimuth telescopes.

Cumming's Finest Hour

Staff Sergeant Frank Cummings was too jumpy to eat the meal that had been brought out by the chow truck to Battery Herring, overlooking the Delaware beach from a scrub-covered dune. His coffee had gone stone cold and the wind had blown his ham sandwich off the toolbox he was using for a table. The sandwich had separated, landing mayonnaise-side down in the dirt but Cummings ignored it.

For the third time in the last hour, he walked the short distance from his six-inch gun platform to the battery bunker's observation slit to ask if anything was being reported from the towers or radars. With more than a hint of annoyance in his voice, Corporal Arthur Fitzhugh replied, through the slit, that he would check once again. Fitzhugh called Tower #6 on the beach, just north of the town of Rehoboth.

An equally annoyed corporal, scanning the ocean with an azimuth telescope from his tower perch, 60 feet above, curtly replied, "Still nothing. But we *will* report if we do see *anything*, Mac." With the field phone handset still to his ear, Fitzhugh gave Cummings his answer by merely shaking his head "no" and raised his binoculars to his eyes, ending the conversation.

Cummings walked the few steps back to his gun and, one more time, counted the ten armor-piercing projectiles and powder bags that had been brought out by his gun crew's Ammunition Squad. It didn't occur to him that the totals were unchanged from the last several counts he had take.

Next, he moved alongside Private Martin Trimper, the gun pointer seated behind the gun's heavy steel shield. "You OK Marty?" Cummings asked him, as much a check on himself as on Trimper. "Yeah Sarge. But we been sittin' here for three hours. How much longer we hafta stay here?" From his seat on the other side of the gun, Private Bobby Cropper chimed in before Cummings could answer, "Yeah, how much longer. I'm cold!" "Till we're relieved dammit; till we're relieved. If the *Krauts* come within range, we gotta be ready to fire." Cummings noted the tension in his own voice as he dried his sweaty palms on his blue dungaree pants, well aware of his elevated pulse and agitated tone.

Cummings' gun platform was in the open air on a dune above beach, just outside the massive Battery Herring concrete bunker. A briny mist reduced the visibility out to sea to three miles. The sky, the ocean and the mist were uniformly grey. He squinted out to sea but not a speck of the horizon was visible. The back of his neck tingled when he considered the possibility of a German spotter watching him through a submarine periscope and directing a battleship broadside right at him. His mouth was so dry that he couldn't swallow as he again replayed in his mind his expectations for an artillery duel with the German fleet.

He wrestled with the reality that the Battery Commander, safe inside the bunker, would excitedly urge his six-inch gun crew to keep firing the 105-pound projectiles as quickly as they could reload and re-point the gun, regardless of any incoming rounds exploding nearby. He knew with certainty he would need to fight the instinctive self-preservation impulse to run for cover, hoping for the courage to stay with the gun and fight. He knew that, unless he stood right next to the young privates on his crew and calmly led them step-by-step, his gun would be out of action and the green kids might even bolt.

He wasn't sure how brave he was going to be himself and, in his imagination, he couldn't picture himself any further through the present situation. Never, in his ten years of laid-back weekend drills in the Delaware National Guard, did the A&P produce manager from Georgetown think he would ever be placed in this dangerous position.

Cummings longed to be at home with his wife and daughter and wondered if they knew what he was doing right then. He suppressed a strong urge to run back to the phone booth outside the Administration Building to call his wife and little girl, in case it was his last chance to speak with them.

The townspeople of Lewes and Rehoboth Beach, Delaware, who were following the German fleet's progress in the news, deduced that the absence of soldiers on pass in the two towns meant that they were probably at battle stations, ready to exchange fire with the powerful German fleet and the word spread like wildfire. Fearing a furious artillery duel that would spill over into the two towns, many loaded their families and what treasured possessions they could grab into cars and farm trucks and fled west, away from the ocean.

At 1036 hours Eastern Standard Time, Colonel Ruhlen read an intelligence report that placed the German fleet 17 miles due east of Atlantic City, New Jersey and headed in his direction. Unable to sit still, the colonel donned his helmet and walked briskly out of his office, instinctively feeling for the .45 hanging on his thigh. Ruhlen hopped into his jeep and drove over to the Battery Smith concrete casemate that housed the fort's two 16-inch guns with the regiment's longest range. Satisfied that the two gun crews were ready and eager to fight, he headed over to the battery's underground plotting room. The Battery Commander, Major Donald Everitt, assured Ruhlen that they were as ready as they could be: the projectile and powder details were fully manned and ready, he was in telephone contact with the battery's azimuth and range readers in the beach towers and everything was in order. "If you gave me a fire mission, "I could hit 'em but remember," Colonel, "we can't see 'em till they're within 14 miles of the beach."[97]

Ruhlen was fully aware of the fire control towers' 14-mile line-of-sight capability but had never before that moment thought of it as a liability. Without a triangulated fix from the towers on the enemy ships, they could almost certainly not be hit by his slow-firing 16- and 12-inch batteries. For the first time, Ruhlen wondered why the towers had not been built taller, affording a view to a more distant horizon. He also remembered that, in an exercise earlier that year, airborne artillery spotting from blimps and observation planes was found to be totally ineffective because the observers could only guess at their own positions, forcing useless estimates of moving target locations.

His thoughts next shifted to how badly Fort Miles was outgunned. His two heaviest batteries, 16-inch Battery Smith and 12-inch Battery 519, which had previously only fired single test shots, could theoretically sustain an unverified rate of fire of only one round per minute from each of their four guns. Intelligence on the German ships worried Ruhlen; 52 big guns capable of firing broadsides twice per minute at his stationary emplacements would turn his beachfront installation into an exploding scene from hell for gun crews in the open air. The colonel's strong sense of his personal call to historic stand-and-fight duty ebbed to an unspoken prayer that the Huns would just keep on going.

---

[97] Fort Miles' fire mission plotting rooms depended on azimuth and range solutions based on visual observations from the towers. The tallest Fort Miles tower afforded only a 14-mile view to the horizon. Knowing that beforehand, the *Kriegsmarine* planners restricted the fleet's approach to no closer than 16 miles.

Wilhelm Metzger the Navigator

From the starboard rail of Destroyer Z16 *Friedrich Eckhold, Kapitanleutenant* Wilhelm Metzger strained for a glimpse of the Delaware coast through his binoculars. As lead navigator for the German fleet underway, Metzger was meticulously plotting the destroyer's position minute-by-minute and had ordered the duty signalman to flash a report by lamp that Z16 had just crossed into the field of fire of Fort Miles' biggest weapons, the twin 16-inch guns of Battery Smith. The signal had been acknowledged by the Battlecruiser *Scharnhorst*, two kilometers astern off Z16's port side.

The young navigator glowed inside with the satisfying thought that his message would be relayed throughout the whole fleet underway and that he was being relied upon by all his comrades from the admiral on down.

Metzger returned to the bridge, walking the few steps back to the chart table and bent again to study the intelligence map of the New Jersey, Delaware, and Maryland coast. The map displayed a 25-mile arc centered on Cape Henlopen, extending offshore to represent the big guns' effective range.

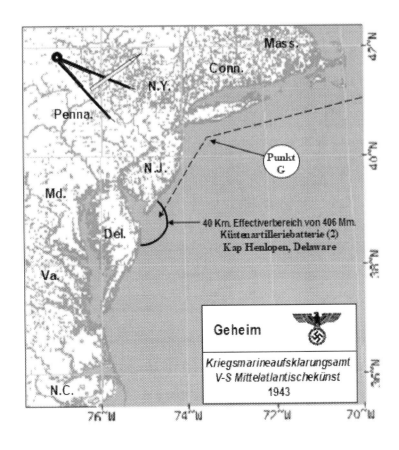

150

Looking at Z16's position just inside the arc, the navigator's earlier confidence suddenly wavered with the realization that now, big American projectiles could reach his ship and blow it to bits. Conscious of a flushed warmth growing from head-to-toe, Metzger looked astern for a moment, and - reassured that mighty *Scharnhorst* was still in position – went back to the starboard rail and resumed his binocular search for land, all the while mindful that from 27 kilometers (17 miles) out, the earth's curvature made the view impossible.

Silently, he reviewed the drill and the math: "If they open fire, I will see the muzzle flashes against the clouds immediately. We will then have only 45 seconds to change course to seaward before their projectiles hit the water. *Kapitän* Vogelmann will immediately order the change of course on my word and he will break radio silence to alert the rest of the fleet. We shan't hear their guns till almost two minutes after they have fired but I may see muzzle flashes again nearly a minute after their first salvo."

The rolling sea challenged Metzger's keeping the heavy binoculars trained on where he believed Fort Miles to be and he thought his heart had stopped when momentary glare flooded his vision. Metzger's throat constricted as he discounted what he believed must have been an illusion and not the expected muzzle flash. Stunned by the momentous decision facing him, he tried unsuccessfully to count off the expected 40 seconds to impact in panicked contemplation that he had failed in his duty.

What seemed an eternity passed without any nearby splashing projectiles, reflected muzzle flashes, or distant rumbles. Paralyzed in time and space, his elbows braced firmly against the rail, Metzger was afraid to shift the aim of his binoculars and stared at a magnified grey horizon until he heard Petty Officer Eschers cry-out that Z16 was crossing out of Fort Miles' 16-inch gun range. If Navigator Metzger could keep to course, the fleet would not be visible from shore and no American guns could reach them for the rest of the cruise.

Jolted back to the present, Metzger shouted, "Make position report to *Scharnhorst*" and moved inside to sit next to the chart table, his back turned to the rest of the bridge crew. He discovered his fingers trembling and sweat breaking out above his upper lip, grateful that no one could see him.

The Crisis Eases

To almost universal relief, the Germans did keep going. Later, a blimp from the Naval Air Station at Weeksville, North Carolina reported the Germans 50 miles south of the Delaware-Maryland line and heading south at an estimated speed of twelve knots. 2nd Coast Artillery District lowered Fort Miles' readiness level to Condition II three hours later. In another two hours, Destroyer Z-16 signaled its arrival at *Punkt Siegfried* [98] and Admiral Lütjens ordered a fleet change of course to 090 degrees, heading due east and away from the US coast. Tensions relaxed on both sides and Lütjens authorized the cruiser *Prinz Eugen* to stop long enough to rendezvous with submarine U-123 for the transfer of a sailor needing an emergency appendectomy. *Korvettenkäpitan* Reinhard Hardegen, the U-Boat's skipper, permitted his broadly-smiling crew to come up into the fresh air and collect produce and movies and to banter with their genuinely affectionate comrades on the cruiser.

Later, over beers in Lewes and Rehoboth, many of the younger 21st Coast Artillery cannoneers bemoaned their missed opportunity to see "action" and reassured each other that they would have sunk every *Kraut* ship they sighted. Pleased with the troops' high morale, George Ruhlen decided not to burst their bubble but he began composing two documents. The first was a recommendation for a unit citation, acknowledging its courageous preparedness for combat. The second was an "After Action Report" to 2nd Coast Artillery District that expressed worried concerns about the limited horizon visible to Fort Miles' fire control towers and the low rate of sustained fire the fort could expect to maintain against an offshore enemy.

Inside the now quiet Battery Herring Bunker, a trembling Sergeant Frank Cummings closed the door of the parts storeroom behind him and, with racking sobs, shed the first salty tears of his adulthood. In a few minutes, his swollen tensions released, the sergeant composed himself and went in search of his gun crew to share a celebratory drink. He never described his concealed fear, claimed his demonstrated courage, or momentary emotional release to anyone but, for the rest of his life, was silently proud of having stayed at his post doing his duty in the face of enormous odds. He knew it was a defining moment of his life.

---

[98] Point "S" in the German phonetic alphabet

Most Americans sighed in reprieve but closed-door sessions in Washington and military headquarters were grim. The US had dodged a bullet but the Germans' close pass revealed an unready capability to assert itself defensively. Already bitterly but resolutely divided, the national security players in the Thomas Administration and both houses of Congress succumbed to dovish versus hawkish finger-pointing recriminations that led to a search for a comprehensive solution that would please everybody. Political considerations displaced and diminished the security issues. No constructive courses of action could be agreed and the crisis ultimately subsided.

Back in Kiel harbor, *Kapitanleutnant* Wilhelm Metzger stood proudly as Admiral Lutjens hung the Iron Cross around his neck, congratulating his distinguished navigating accomplishment. Forever proud of his role in guiding the historic cruise and a frequent attendee at shipmate reunions but sobered by the reality of confronting gripping fear, Metzger took his private, unrevealed memory to his grave after a comfortable retirement.

End Notes, References and Photo Credits

Author Contact:

Referring to myself as "the author" is unnecessarily stuffy. "I" is better.

I welcome comments, questions, and alternative views, which may be emailed to me at: *SheffordPress@ earthlink.net.*

Preface, Foreword, and Introduction

The assertion that the National World War 2 Memorial omits the Coast Artillery' front-line service immediately after the Pearl Harbor attack was confirmed by the National Park Service in 2008 and again in 2021.

Camp Henlopen was renamed Fort Miles by an Act of Congress in honor of the late Lieutenant General Nelson Appleton Miles.

The site cost $22 million to build and covered 1,155 acres, including four miles of ocean beach front and a one-mile strip of beach along the bay. Delaware State officials report that all the towers are safe, even the ones at ocean's edge next to Gordon's Pond, because their concrete foundations were set atop creosote-soaked wood pilings driven deep into the sand.

<u>Soldier's Oath, US Army</u>

> I, (name), do solemnly swear (or affirm) that I will support and defend the Constitution
> of the United States against all enemies, foreign and domestic; that I will bear true
> faith and allegiance to the same; and that I will obey the orders of the President of
> the United States and the orders of the officers appointed over me, according to
> regulations and the Uniform Code of Military Justice. So help me God.

I, (name), do solemnly swear (or affirm) that I will support and defend the Constitution of the United States and the State of Delaware against all enemies, foreign and domestic; that I will bear true faith and allegiance to the same; and that I will obey the orders of the President of the United States and the Governor of Delaware and the orders of the officers appointed over me, according to law and regulations. So help me God.

FDR's and Mrs. Roosevelt's post-Pearl Harbor concerns about a west coast invasion and the Secret Service's timed wheelchair evacuation are documented in Doris Kearns Goodwin's, *No Ordinary Time: Franklin and Eleanor Roosevelt – the Home Front in WW2.*

Photo Credits:

- In the Foreword - Troops coming out of shelter: Official US Army photo in the Library of Congress
- In the Introduction: World War 2 Memorial - Author

Chapter 1, The Pre-Pearl Harbor Strategic World Setting

The assertion that the "perceptions of many Americans" about the date World War 2 began, is based on the results of an informal questionnaire asking for the dates of principal US conflicts since the War for American Independence. For World War 2, most respondents wrote "1941-1945." A very few wrote "1939" or "1938" and a surprising number of both mature and youthful respondents wrote starting dates past the 1940s.

The official 1939 analysis that suggested heavy German ships might be able to shell US coastal assets from positions outside the range of Army Coast Artillery guns, identified an issue that was not satisfactorily resolved by Fort Miles' fire control tower and big gun design. All of the fort's assets were in fixed locations surely known to the *Kriegsmarine* with some small degree of error. Heavy German ships, maneuvering off the Delaware coast beyond the visible horizon (i.e., further than fifteen miles), could shell Fort Miles installations without being seen from the fort or its beachfront towers. "Blind" broadsides fired from sea at calculated fort positions, very probably would have caused explosive near-misses resulting in at least some, perhaps much damage and casualties. "Over- the-horizon" bombardment, directed by observation aircraft known to be carried by some German ships, could have greatly improved the accuracy of the ships' guns. As in the example of the 1942 submarine shelling near Santa Barbara, where no Coast Artillery guns could respond, the 1939 findings were probably still applicable to coastal Delaware in 1941-42.

The uniform badge shown on the last page of Chapter 1 was adopted as the insignia of the 261st Coast Artillery Regiment of the Delaware National Guard. When the unit was federalized, it was reformed as a brigade, an echelon lower than regiment.

The source for the August 1941 labor strike is the *Salisbury (MD) Times* of August 28, 1941.

Photo Credits:

- Cape May Canal – Author
- MV *Pinguin* – Library of Congress
- Lt. Colonel Roscoe – Delaware Parks & Recreation
- *Schleswig-Holstein* in Danzig harbor – Government of Poland Archives
- Delaware National Guard Flag – State of Delaware
- Tent City – Official US Army photo in the Library of Congress
- 8-inch railway gun – US Army ROTC Training Manual, Coast Artillery, Basic

Reference:

Cohen and DeNevi, *They Came to Destroy America*, 2003: Missoula MT, Pictorial Histories Publishing Company, provides text and photo illustrations of movements in the US sympathetic to German *Nazis*.

Chapter 2, An Anxious Defense Outlook

Sector General Order Number 1, assigning Fort Miles responsibility for its own defense against seaborne landings, stated: "The Mobile Forces allotted to Sectors are for the primary purpose of defense against landing operations by establishing outposts, outside the Harbor Defenses, covering the likely landing areas, and patrolling between such outposts and the harbor defenses themselves. They will not be assigned to the local defenses of nor as reinforcements for Harbor Defenses except in emergencies."

In *Fire Control and Direction for Coast Artillery (1907)*, then Colonel Clint C. Hearn of the US Army Signal School wrote, "It is important, then, whenever our relations with a foreign power become strained, to take active measures to put our coast defenses in such a state of preparedness as will effectually check these early attempts [as raids during the earliest stages of a war]."

War stories persist about German submariners, taken prisoner when their U-Boats were captured, who had US movie ticket stubs and grocery receipts in their pockets. The inference of these stories is that those submariners had been on surreptitious "shore leave" under the noses of US military authorities and local seaboard populations. One such story has been recently published in *More Stories from Delaware Bay* collected by J. Hanna (2002: Cherokee Books). Citing unnamed sources, the legend is retold of a Delaware Bay shellfish dredger that was boarded inside the bay by a party from a German U-Boat, who seized their fresh water, food, and whiskey. According to Hanna's unnamed source, the victims were not believed when they reported the boarding. Former German U-Boat skipper Reinhard Hardegen debunked these and similar stories in a post-war interview.

The German Navy only laid down one ship that could be considered a fleet aircraft carrier. This was the *Graf Zeppelin*, launched in December 1936 but never commissioned. She was never fully completed and spent most of her life being moved from port to port to protect her from air attack. After the war, *Graf Zeppelin* was taken over by the Soviets and sunk as a target. The only other project in the works was the planned conversion of a heavy cruiser to an aircraft carrier. The cruiser *Siletz* was selected but Allied bombing, German lack of resources and manpower kept this ship from being completed for wartime service. The website http://en2.wikipedia.org/ wiki/German_ aircraft_carrier_ Graf_Zeppelin provides additional interesting details.

The source for "caretaker status" of US Atlantic coast defenses is *1930 Reorganization and New Training Objective of CAC*, CA Journal Vol. 72, pp 1-11.

Photo Credits:

- R. Hardegen – Library of Congress

- Admiral King - Official US Navy photo in the Library of Congress

- Stuka – Copy of an illustration by Douglas Rolfe, *Airplanes of the World*, 1954: New York, Simon and Schuster drawn by Tom Kramer

- Inbound Freighter – National Archives (photo modified by addition of superimposed signal flags)

- 8-inch railway gun - Official US Army photo in the Library of Congress

References:

Cohen and DeNevi, *They Came to Destroy America*, 2003: Missoula MT, Pictorial Histories Publishing Company. A well-documented source for the landings of German saboteurs on east coast beaches.

Various websites found by searching for keywords, such as "Battle of Los Angeles."

Chapter 3, Enemy Threats and Fort Miles Capabilities

Contemporary maps – some formerly classified – prepared by the Office of the Artillery Engineer, Harbor Defenses of the Delaware, provided some source material for the locations and coverage of Fort Miles' and Cape May's guns, radars, mines, searchlights, and underwater listening devices. These are on file at the US Army Artillery Museum at Aberdeen Proving Grounds, Maryland.

The heights of the Delaware towers, the heights above ground of their observation slits, the numbers of observation instruments, and the batteries supported by each tower are taken from an unpublished paper written by Beth Ross and provided by the administrative office of Cape Henlopen State Park.

The principal purpose of the towers was to obtain a longer-range view than was available at ground level. Since a tower of sixty to seventy feet provides even longer range observation, if it stands on high ground, the heights of all the towers is given in Chapter 3 as overall heights above sea level. 92. These overall heights were obtained by taking GPS elevation measurements at each of the towers' bases. In some cases (most notably Towers #5 and 6), where the former 1940s ground level is currently unknown because of beach erosion, the accompanying text so states.

The heights of the two towers in Cape May, New Jersey are based on GPS elevation measurements at their bases and an estimate of the towers' heights above ground. Some towers information was obtained from http://ca.ckwinfo.net/dr/miles and from an article in the *Washington Post*, The Mystery Towers, August 26, 1997. The height of Tower #7 at Fort Miles is given at *www.newszap.com* as stretching to 135 feet [above sea level]. GPS measurements taken in 2004 indicate the top of Tower #7 to be 110 feet above sea level.

The text and illustrations in US Army Coast Artillery Field Manual (FM) 4-60, *Service of the Piece 12-inch gun*, were adapted to explain gun crew duties in Chapter 3.

A November 1989 CDSG article, *Seacoast Artillery Radar 1938-46*, by Danny R. Malone, provided selected details for the radar discussion in Chapter 3. Mr. Malone's article is an excellent source for further reading.

Reminiscences of SCR-296 Radar Operations, by Roma Saltzgiver, a Coast Artillery radar officer, are at *http://209.165.152.119/abercrombie/abercrom.html.* This site presents a verbal history interview of Mr. Saltzgiver that was used as a source of SCR-296 information.

A typical SCR radar antenna of the early 1940s, in this case an SCR-270, which was larger than the SCR-296's six-foot by six-foot antenna. (Official US Army photo).

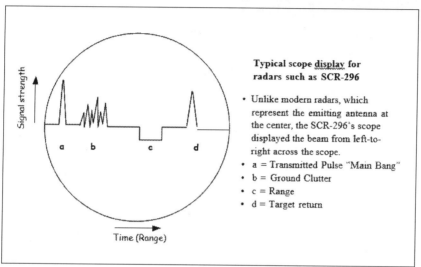

Typical scope display for radars such as SCR-296

- Unlike modern radars, which represent the emitting antenna at the center, the SCR-296's scope displayed the beam from left-to-right across the scope.
- a = Transmitted Pulse "Main Bang"
- b = Ground Clutter
- c = Range
- d = Target return

Drawing contributed by Elliot Deutsch/CDSG

The addition of IFF (meaning "Identification Friend or Foe") on military radars began very early in the development of radar systems. However, IFF depends upon the receipt and recognition of an identifying transmission from a friendly ship or aircraft. This reaction by an on-board transponder is triggered automatically when the transponder receives and recognizes the radar signal. The IFF concept is that a ship or aircraft "painted" by friendly radar that does not respond with the expected IFF transmission, is presumed to be a foe. In 1941-42, there was no radar capability at Fort Miles. In 1943, when the first of the SCR-296 radars were installed, what few IFF transponders existed in the US inventory, were installed on military aircraft as protection against being fired on by friendly AAA guns. Nearly no vessels of the Navy, Coast Guard, or commercial shipping companies would have been equipped with IFF at this very early date.

On aerial reconnaissance of the sea approaches: It is instructive to note that, in May 1938, roughly three and one-half years before the US entry into World War 2, the world was astounded by a seemingly impossible feat of aerial navigation: US Army Air Corps B-17s, led by Curtis LeMay, located the Italian liner *Rex* 700 miles out in the Atlantic and dropped a greeting message on her deck. This bit of "aviation firsts" lore underscores the widely-perceived difficulty of the time in (1) fixing an aircraft's own position with precision and (2) locating a ship at sea, out of sight of land. The US Navy was simultaneously embarrassed and incensed at LeMay's apparently exacting navigation skills and his publicly predicting the vulnerability of naval ships to attack from the air. Strong complaints by surface ship admirals to the War Department actually resulted in a restriction of Air Corps sorties to no more than 100 miles off the east coast. In reality, Le May found the Rex by homing-in on her ship-to-shore radio transmissions and then finally seeing her wake. Against a German ship maintaining radio silence, the result would have surely been much different. In actuality, there was no dependable capability for finding enemy ships at sea in the 1940s, if they observed radio silence

US Army Technical Manual (TM) 5-7144 was used as a source of information for 60-inch searchlights.

Records Group 392 for the US Coast Artillery (Block 01-42) for the years 1901 to 1950 at the National Archives preserves original documents of the 21st Coast Artillery Regiment and its parent organizations.

The One Hundred Year History of the Pilots' Association Bay and River Delaware (1996: Delaware Heritage Press) provided the first-person reminiscences of 1940s pilots.

Photo Credits:

- Two cannoneers on 155mm – Official US Army photo in the Library of Congress
- Torpedo Service sleeve and cloth insignia – hand drawn by Tom Kramer
- Mineplanter - Official US Army photo in the Library of Congress
- M-4 Mine - Official US Army photo in the Library of Congress
- Watercolor of Mine Planting ship – Painted by Schroeder in 1943; the print is in the Library of Congress
- Mine control panels – Delaware Parks and Recreation
- Searchlight crew - Official US Army photo in the Library of Congress

- Tower conduits – Author

- All other tower photos and views in and from towers – Author

- All casemates and bunkers – Author

- Restored 16-inch and 3-inch guns and shells – Author

- 155mm gun and crew - Official US Army photo in the Library of Congress

- 8-inch and 6-inch guns – Author

- Mine Dock – Author

- Collapsed USCG Station – National Archives and Records Administration

- 6-inch Shield Gun - Official US Army photo in the Library of Congress

- 16-inch guns in casemates - Official US Army photos in the Library of Congress

- 12-inch gun in casemate – author

- 12-inch projectile store room - Official US Army photo in the Library of Congress

Chapter 4, The Cannoneers' Operational Challenge

Explanation of the quotation marks on "Flat": "Flat" Trajectories are differentiated from high-arcing trajectories. The laws of physics cause an unpowered ballistic object in motion to be pulled constantly toward the Earth by the force of gravity. As a term used in artillery, "flat" has a connotation that is relative to trajectories of high arcs. A truly "flat" trajectory is a physical impossibility for an artillery shell fired at a target mile away.

The peak muzzle velocity of a large artillery piece is achieved some milliseconds after the powder bags snugly behind the projectile have exploded, accelerating the projectile forward. Optimally, all the powder explodes while the projectile is still moving within the gun tube to achieve maximum forward speed.

As an example, a 16-in gun with a muzzle velocity of 2700 feet per second can send a projectile 44,000 yards or 132,000 feet or 25 miles (132,000 ÷ 5280 feet per mile = 25 miles). At 2700 feet per second, the quickest a projectile could travel 25 miles would be 48.8 seconds but that would be a shortest-distance, straight line of 25 miles and assumes that the projectile does not decelerate after exiting the gun tube.

Numerous factors complicate determining precisely when a projectile will hit the point where aimed. To achieve the 25-mile range, the 16-inch gun tube must be elevated, sending the projectile thousands of feet up in the air on a long arcing trajectory, adding substantial time between firing and impact. However, the projectile's acceleration immediately ends when it leaves the gun tube and the following super-hot explosive gas that was pushing it dissipates in the open air.

Once free of the gun tube, the projectile immediately begins decelerating from its peak velocity (2700 feet per second) all the way up to the highest point (apogee) of the arc and then accelerates as it falls back to earth but does not reach the original peak velocity.

Wind, barometric pressure, and humidity, which may be different at the various altitudes crossed by the projectile in flight, can also affect the elapsed time between firing and impact. The purpose of this discussion focuses on principles and scenarios without applying complicated mathematical variables.

Interested readers will find websites and books in technical libraries that provide formulas for artillery trajectory calculations as well as ready-made "look-up" tables. One source for calculating the flight time of an artillery projectile, using muzzle velocity and elevation of the gun barrel is given at *http://hypertextbook.com/facts/2002/ NickishaBerlus.shtml*.

The "Shot on Way" emblem of the 261st Coast Artillery Regiment is available as a full-color pin from the Fort Miles Historical Association (*www.fmha.org*). All proceeds support the Coast Artillery Museum in Cape Henlopen State Park and the restoration of the fire control towers.

Underlying math for the discussion on how many projectiles Fort Miles and Cape May could have put into a target area within ten miles of the beach:

Gun	Rounds per minute	Number of Guns	Gun/Rounds per Minute
16-inch	1	2	2
12-inch	1.5	2	3
8-inch	1.5	8	12
155mm	4	8	32
6-inch	4	6	24
3-inch/90mm	5.5	8	44
Total rounds per minute from all batteries			117
Total rounds per second from all batteries			~ 2

The source for the account of Leonard Millar's observation of 16-inch projectile impacts off the New Jersey coast is *www.newszap.com.*

Text and illustrations in US Army Technical Manuals (TMs) 9-2681 for Plotting Boards M-3 and M-4 and TM 9-2683 for Plotting Board M-5 were used to explain the use of the boards at Fort Miles and to create the accompanying illustration in Chapter 4. Figure 4-5 is adapted from the US Army ROTC Manual on Coast Artillery and has been simplified.

The Army Training Manual on *Fire Control and Positioning for Seacoast Artillery* is the source of the "stack and stick" method of classifying potential ship targets.

On timing bells: It was obviously important to know precisely which targets were the subjects of azimuths reported by observers in the towers. A related problem addressed by the US Navy was knowing which ship's guns had caused miss-splashes when more than one US ship was firing at a single enemy target ship. The problem was solved by including dyes in the artillery projectiles that actually colored the splashes. No references to the Coast Artillery's use of colored miss-splashes were found. I welcome reader comments.

Photo Credits:

- 14-mile horizon from tower – Author

- Ten members of a gun crew - Official US Army photo in the Library of Congress

- Tracker and Reader using Azimuth Instrument - Official US Army photo published by the State of Maine Bureau of Parks and Lands on its website.

- Depression instrument - Official US Army photo in the Library of Congress

- Meteorological Section - Official US Army photo in the Library of Congress

- Battery switchboard operator - Official US Army photo in the Library of Congress

- Field telephone - Official US Army photo in the Library of Congress

- Reenactors manning Plotting Board in Fort Miles Museum - Author

Chapter 5, Soldiering at Wartime Fort Miles

References:

Fort Miles weekly newspapers *Time Table* and *Coastal Bursts* Seek Publishing, *1942: Remember When*

2002: Arcadia Publishing, *Delaware in World War 2* presents very good photos of troops at Fort Miles and 1940s life in nearby towns.

Photo Credits:

- American Campaign Medal – Library of Congress

- 21st CAR troops - Official US Army photo in the Library of Congress

- Bugler - Official US Army photo in the Library of Congress

- Ration stamps – author

- Sgt. C. West - Official US Army photo in the Library of Congress

- Chaplain Bishop - Official US Army photo in the Library of Congress

- Coca-Cola cooler – National Archives and Records Administration

- Shower and Latrine – Delaware Parks and Recreation

Chapter 6, Fort Miles Stands Down

On telephones: By 21st century contemporary standards, the communications support available for command and control of the Coast Artillery mission at Fort Miles was primitive and "soft." Photographs of reinforced concrete casemates housing heavy weapons show flimsy pole-mounted telephone cables in the open air. These vital lines would have been at severe risk of destruction had enemy projectiles exploded near the casemates, even if no damage had been done to casemates and their contents. Cannoneers behind sandbags (often paper sacks of cement allowed to absorb rainwater and harden) at open-air positions were equally dependent on telephone lines to receive direction from their battery plotting rooms. The loss of the tactical telephone system, which might also be caused by loss of its power supply or the fragile switchboards in use, would have forced falling back to VHF "walkie-talkie" radios, which were far less user-friendly, reliable, and intelligible than telephones.

Ironically, the 261st Coast Artillery had its first and only actual contact with a Kriegsmarine vessel, U-858. This submarine, as was true of the 261st, had no combat engagements during the war. U-858 "struck-out" on its two wartime cruises and claimed no Allied ships sunk or damaged. www.uboat. net/boats/u858.htm and www.subvets.org/news/subhist.htm.

On the "furlough atmosphere" at Fort Miles: An informational sign erected by Cape Henlopen State Park near the park's fishing pier (old World War 2 mine dock) states: "Life at Fort Miles was unexciting."

Photo Credit:

- Discharge photo: Delaware Public Archives
- About gun carriages: A specialized sub-section of fixed-site artillery history concentrates on gun mounts or "carriages." A comprehensive discussion supported by the necessary illustrations would consume many pages and is not included here. The reader should be aware, however, that one of the benefits of certain gun carriages over available others was the accommodation of higher angles of gun tube elevation, which extended the gun's range.

For example, the ability provided by a redesigned carriage to raise a 6-inch gun to a maximum elevation of 46 degrees increased its range from 9 to 15 miles. Additional detailed discussion and data on various gun carriages has been documented by the Coast Defense Study Group (CDSG) and other writers on many Internet websites.

U-858's black surrender flag – In 2002, U-858's Engineer Officer, Karl Heinz Barr, visited Cape Henlopen State Park and toured the former Fort Miles installations. Dr. Gary Wray, President of the Fort Miles Historical Association, was Herr Barr's escort and quotes Herr Barr as declaring that U-858 had been ordered to fly a black and not a white flag for their surrender. Obedient to the end, even in defeat, the captain of U-858 complied.

Photo Credits:

- World War 2 Victory Medal – Library of Congress
- 1945: Fort Miles' first discharged soldiers – Delaware Parks and Recreation
- Reenactor gun crew - Delaware Parks and Recreation

Annex A, US Coast Defenses in World War 2

Photo Credits:

- AAA gun – official US Army photo
- Towed 155mm gun – official US Army photo
- Tower at Pulpit Rock – Bob LaFlamme
- Tower at Fort Pickens – Andy Bennett
- Towers at Fort Foster and Virginia Beach – Pete & Phil Payette, American Forts Network
- Towers at Miller Field, Shadmoor Park, and Montauk – Richard Parker
- Tower at Battery Strong/San Diego – National Park Service
- Fort Dumpling/Rhode Island – Town of Jamestown
- Two towers in New Brunswick – Parks Canada
- Tower at Felixstowe – Suffolk Coastal District Council, UK
- German tower on Alderney – Nick Catford

- Church in Colville - author

Chapter 7, Signature Icons of the Delaware Seashore

Photo Credits:

- Miniature tower – author
- Shirt – author
- Billboard - author

Annex D, Two Alternative History Scenarios

The illustration is a German World War 2 propaganda poster, translating to "Sortie of the Navy." A copy is in the Library of Congress.

Annex D-1, A German Attack on Wilmington

The "what-if" scenario described in Annex D-1 is completely fictitious and is of the literary genre known as "Alternative History," which is historical fiction with a twist. Plausibility distinguishes alternative history from fanciful science fiction and readers are free to judge whether the "what-if" German attack on Wilmington in December 1941 was plausible, based on the level of combat readiness of the US in general and the Coast Artillery in particular.

Photo Credits:

- Admiral Räder – Library of Congress
- Two destroyers – a composite using file images in the Library of Congress

Annex D-2, "Provocative Cruise of the Iron Fleet"

The annex is totally fictitious.

- In the fictitious story, Lütjens was authorized to resort to arms if American warships tried to prevent the fleet from exercising their right of way in international waters. Actually, before

Germany declared war on the US in December 1941, *Kriegsmarine* Admiral Räder said that German naval forces would ". . . if need be, resort to arms if American warships should try" to prevent them from exercising their right" to sink enemy merchant ships." Räder also complained about the American patrol system and hinted that American communication to the British of the positions of German naval units might be treated as an act of war. [http://www.nationarchive.com/Summaries/v152i0022_03.htm].

- *Korvettenkäpitan* Reinhard Hardegen was actually the skipper of U-123 and, in 1942, actually did surface the sub close enough to New York City to permit his crew to come up on deck to see the city's lights.

Actual fates of the German ships named in the story:

Ship	Fate
Battleship *Bismarck*	Sunk in the North Atlantic in 1940 by Royal Navy warships and carrier-based aircraft. Admiral Lütjens went down with her.
Battleship *Tirpitz*	Sunk by the Royal Air Force in Tromsø Fjord, Norway in 1944 with 5.4 ton "Tallboy" bombs.
Battlecruiser *Graf Spee*	Trapped in Uruguay harbor, where she had gone to make repairs, scuttled in 1939 by its crew off the coast to avoid capture.
Battlecruiser *Deutschland*	Sunk by the Royal Air Force off Swinemunde by 5.4 ton Tallboy bombs in April 1945
Battlecruiser *Scharnhorst*	Sunk in the North Atlantic by Royal Navy warships in 1943
Battlecruiser *Prinz Eugen*	Survived World War II; surrendered to the Allies in Copenhagen in 1945
Battlecruiser *Gniesenau*	Struck a mine and was undergoing repairs in Kiel when sunk by the Royal Air Force in 1942
Destroyer Z17 *von Roeder*	Sunk at Narvik in 1941
Destroyer Z16 *Friedrich Eckhold*	Sunk in 1942
Yacht *Sachsenhausen*	Fictitious

But – while the annex is totally fictitious - about the invented and very complicated "what-if" scenario in which Japanese Admiral Chuichi Nagumo fully executes the plan for neutralizing the US Pacific fleet and repeatedly launches successive crippling air strikes instead of withdrawing back to Japan after only a single raid. In 2008, both Former House of Representatives Newt Gingrich and I both published Alternative History books based on that premise exactly. The Speaker's book is *"Days of Infamy"* and my book is *"At Least I Know I'm Free."* The Alternative History in this annex proceeds from the premise that the US did not fight in World War 2, leaving Germany to dominate Europe and pressure the US economically and militarily. The content of Annex D-2 here is extracted from *At Least I Know I'm Free* [ISBN 0-7414-4036-9]

May 3, 2008, Annapolis, Maryland: Former House of Representatives Speaker Newt Gingrich and Bill Grayson exchange copies of their most recent books, Speaker Gingrich's "Days of Infamy" and Grayson's "At Least I Know I'm Free."

Photo Credit

Speaker Gingrich and author – Shirley Grayson

Index

M

Millar, Leonard 70, 165
Mine Battery 12, 39, 41, 42, 58
Minefields 29, 40, 41, 42, 78, 84
Mine Planter 39, 40
Mine Planting Service 39
Missouri, Battleship 38
MIT 43

O

Operation Pastorius 25
Operation Pelican 24

P

Project Bumblebee 101

R

Radar 12, 17, 29, 42, 43, 44, 45, 46, 47, 48, 53, 55,
    59, 68, 70, 73, 80, 101, 111, 112, 144, 145, 146,
    147, 159, 160, 161
Rader, Erich 131
Railway guns 8, 28, 32, 157, 159
Riggin, Ed Sr 93
Roosevelt, Franklin D. 1, 139
Roscoe, Henry K. 5
Ruhlen, George 12, 146, 152

S

Saltzgiver, Roma 45, 160
Schleswig-Holstein, Battleship 6
SCR- 43, 80
Searchlights v, xii, 12, 29, 46, 48, 49, 50, 53, 55, 56,
    58, 59, 111, 112, 125, 135, 138, 146, 159, 162
Smith, Bill 25, 26
SOSUS 102
Stimson, Henry 19
Stuka 24, 159

T

Time-Interval Bell 82
Torpedo Service 39, 162
Trader, Ralph 4, 96
Truman, Harry S. xii

U

USS Arizona 103

W

Wheeler, Dr. Dean vii
White Construction Co. 7
Wildwood Beach, NJ 48, 50, 65, 70, 71
World War 2 Victory Medal 100, 168
Wray, Dr. Gary vi, 103, 168

About the Author

William C. Grayson

Military historian Bill Grayson is formally trained as a USAF Intelligence Officer. He served as Commander and as Operations Officer of Air Force Signals Intelligence, Counterintelligence, and Operations Security units in Europe and South Vietnam, and served three tours at the National Security Agency as a Cryptologic Staff Officer and as the Chief of Transmission Security overseeing all DoD joint service programs. After completing his Air Force career, Bill joined the US Department of Commerce as a Telecommunications Specialist securing the computers and communications of whole federal civil agencies across the US and in Latin America.

Following his service at Commerce, Bill was a Senior Security Engineering Consultant with leading aerospace defense contractors and was Principal Engineer at Federally Funded R&D Contractors in Washington. In that capacity he was an Information Systems security architect of very large computer networks of NASA, and the Defense, Treasury, Justice, and Transportation Departments and performed special activities for the White House, Air Force One, the Joint Chiefs of Staff, NATO and the Nuclear Regulatory Commission. In support of Homeland Security, he supported US Coast Guard Port Vulnerability studies on all three coasts and contributed to a White House study of the distribution of intelligence among federal, state, local, and tribal jurisdictions. .Bill holds BA and MS degrees and is a student of six foreign languages. He is a Certified Computer Systems Security Professional, an Operations Security Certified Professional, and has completed the requirements for professionalization in Communications Security. Bill is a member of the Coast Defense Study Group, the Fort Miles Historical Association, the Air Force Association, the American Legion, Veterans of Foreign Wars, the Freedom Through Vigilance

Association, Vietnam Veterans of America, RAF Chicksands Alumni, the Military Officers Association, and the NSA Phoenix Society. He is an appointed member of his hometown's Public Safety Committee. Bill lives and works in the Maryland suburbs of Washington and is a frequent visitor to the Delaware seashore.

Printed in the United States
by Baker & Taylor Publisher Services